ANTIQUES

THEIR RESTORATION AND PRESERVATION

ANTIQUES
THEIR RESTORATION AND PRESERVATION

A. LUCAS
O.B.E., F.I.C.

Originally published by
EDWARD ARNOLD & CO
This edition published by
CEDRIC CHIVERS LTD
PORTWAY BATH
1970

First Published 1924

This edition published and bound by Cedric Chivers Ltd., Portway, Bath. 1970
at the request of the London & Home Counties Branch of the Library Association
by arrangement with the copyright holder.
Reproduced and Printed by
Redwood Press Limited, Trowbridge & London.

REFACE

...ng with methods of treating
...a view to their restoration
...y scanty, and all that exists
...e few books and pamphlets
...iography at the end of the
...r with occasional scattered
...urnals and brief notes in
...The author, therefore, who
...y of the subject, and who
...helping with the cleaning
...preservation of the objects from the tomb of Tut-ankh-Amen, has ventured to write a small book in the hope that it may be useful to archæologists, museum curators, collectors and others. The book is admittedly elementary, and the author has endeavoured to be as simple and non-technical as possible. He has also tried to be definite, and where there are a number of different methods to indicate the best. It must be remembered, however, that no one remedy can be of universal application and that each case should be treated as a separate and special study, and, in order that this may be done, the underlying

principles are fully explained. The methods recommended are neither difficult nor expensive.

A certain amount of repetition has been unavoidable, as many of the subjects overlap one another.

Some of the instructions and cautions given may possibly appear trivial and unnecessary, but experience proves that many of them are frequently neglected.

In order to save needless repetition, the nature and strength of the materials and solutions recommended for use are described all together at the end of the book.

The common chemical names in ordinary use, whenever they are not wrong, have been employed in preference to others that, although more technically correct, are less well known.

The author wishes to express his thanks and indebtedness to many friends who have generously helped him out of the abundance of their knowledge and experience. The usual references are given in those instances in which methods previously described are referred to.

A. L.

CONTENTS

CHAPTER I
RESTORATION

CHAPTER II
PRESERVATION

CHAPTER III
APPLICATION OF METHODS TO SPECIFIC MATERIALS

CHAPTER IV

SIMPLE PHYSICAL AND CHEMICAL TESTS

CHAPTER I

RESTORATION

The work of restoring and preserving
antique objects naturally divides itself into
two parts : first, the methods, and second,
their application.

The methods are scientific and largely
chemical. The underlying principles are,
firstly, to ascertain of what material the object
to be dealt with is composed, and secondly,
to determine the nature of any change or
deterioration that has taken place; but, in
order to apply this information, there must
be, in addition, a knowledge of the properties
of materials. On these data is based the
appropriate treatment necessary to restore
the object as far as possible to its original
condition and to prevent the occurrence of
any decay, or if decay is already present, to
arrest its further progress and to prevent its
recurrence.

It may seem a very simple matter to
ascertain of what material an object is

1

composed and, in this connection, the knowledge of other and similar objects, gained as the result of experience, is very helpful, but it is not always so simple as it appears and, in spite of experience, archæology is full of mistakes that have been made in the past. If the nature of materials is not simple, the nature of the changes and decay that have taken place is still less simple. With care, however, and by means of a few elementary physical and chemical tests gross errors on both points may be avoided, and methods of testing will therefore be given. But, as already stated, something more than this is required if serious mistakes in treatment are to be avoided; thus, for instance, it might be ascertained that a particular vase was made of alabaster (calcite) and that a crystalline efflorescence on the surface was common salt, but before this information could be usefully applied to the cleaning of the object, it must also be known that alabaster is acted upon by acid, but not by water, and that salt is soluble in water, but not in acid. This knowledge would result in the choice of water and the avoidance of acid for cleaning purposes.

Although the principles on which the restoration and preservation of antiquities are based demand a considerable amount of scientific and chemical knowledge, the application of these principles is largely a matter of skilled manipulation founded upon long training and improved by constant practice. At one time all work of the nature of that under consideration was undertaken without scientific advice, but now the tendency is often in the other direction, and the chemist is expected, not only to evolve methods, but also to carry them out. The most satisfactory arrangement, however, is to have a trained staff of skilled workmen with a consulting chemist, who has specialized in the subject, attached, and every large museum should possess such a staff. For small museums, however, and for work outside museums this is not possible, and the archæologist in the field, the curator of a small museum and the collector must themselves undertake a large part of any restoration work required, and it is for these especially that the present book has been written.

With respect to field work it should be recognized that this must necessarily be only preliminary and in certain cases even crude, owing to the conditions under which it is carried out, namely, absence of suitable accommodation and proper appliances and lack of time. This being the case, field work should be limited to what is sufficient to enable the objects to be photographed, described, and, more particularly, packed and transported in safety. Detailed and final restoration work can only be satisfactorily carried out in a fully equipped workshop and by trained and experienced men, acting under the direction of the expert. Much, however, can now be done in the field that formerly was thought to be impossible, and therefore was not attempted, and there are few objects, no matter of what kind, or how poor their condition, that cannot be preserved, and no object should be condemned as hopeless until it has been carefully studied and preliminary experiments made, since much that may appear at first sight to be beyond salvation can generally be consolidated and improved to at least some extent.

Methods of restoring and preserving antique objects have been practised for so long that it might seem impossible for any that are not at least fairly satisfactory to have persisted, but they do persist, and some which are not only useless, but harmful, are still employed and recommended. This is because such methods give results that appear successful for the time being, and observations are not made, or not recorded, to show the condition of the objects after the lapse of some years.

Before proceeding to details three further points may be mentioned : firstly, the necessity for full publicity in respect to methods ; secondly, the responsibility of the work ; and thirdly, the pleasure of the work. In scientific work there should be no secrets, and details of processes found satisfactory should be communicated freely. This unfortunately is not always done. The work is delicate, and the responsibility great, and a little haste, carelessness or lack of knowledge may irreparably damage an object of beauty and value that cannot be replaced.

The pleasure of the work needs to be known to be fully appreciated, but it is a real joy to see an object that has entered the workshop dirty, corroded and ugly gradually improving and finally becoming clean, healthy and beautiful.

Restoration

The first step in restoration is cleaning, and this therefore will now be considered.

Cleaning Manifestly the first thing to be done is to remove superficial dust and dirt. This may usually be effected by the use of a small pair of bellows or a camel-hair or similar small soft brush. A duster should never be employed, partly because what is happening underneath cannot be seen and followed, and partly because a duster is at best a clumsy instrument and may cause damage by catching in corners or in delicate portions of a carving or in loose pieces of inlay, gilt, or paint.

After blowing or brushing off the loose dust, any more adherent dirt may generally be removed by means of water, petroleum spirit, or alcohol. The simplest reagent, namely water, should be tried first, unless it is manifestly unsuitable.

The nature of the object determines whether water should be employed sparingly or plentifully. In the former case it should be applied by means of a small piece of sponge or a small camel-hair or other similar soft brush, and for small pieces of inlay and for corners by means of a tuft of cotton-wool on the end of a small piece of wood, such as a match with the head removed, or a wooden toothpick. Each time the sponge, brush or cotton-wool is removed from the object it should be rinsed in clean water before being used again, the water being frequently renewed. When water is applied in quantity the object should be immersed and well soaked. In all cases warm water is better than cold.

When washing, it should be remembered that to wash a large number of times with a small quantity of water each time gives better and quicker results than to wash a few times with a large quantity of water. This is a well-known fact, which may be demonstrated chemically and proved mathematically. The rule therefore for all washing is to wash frequently with a little water, though always a sufficiency, rather than to wash a few times with a large amount of water.

Before using water it must be certain that it will not have any injurious effects. This will be known as a rule from the nature of the material or from previous experience, or may be ascertained by means of an experiment on one corner of the object or on a less important object of similar kind. The effects of water on various materials will be described later when dealing with the materials separately, but a few general rules will now be given, to all of which, of course, there may be exceptions. These rules are as follows :

1. Articles of faience, glass and pottery, and in some instances stone, may all be washed safely, and generally need prolonged soaking in repeated changes of water. Faience, pottery and stone, however, all of which are very porous and are liable to contain salt, should never be wetted unless they can be thoroughly soaked, otherwise when the object dries again the salt will be brought to the surface, where it will crystallize and cause damage.

2. Articles of wood should not be wetted unless the wood is hard and in good condition, in which case they may be cleaned with a damp sponge.

3. A painted surface should never be wetted unless it is varnished or has been protected by special treatment. A painted and varnished object will generally bear sponging.

4. Ivory, if in good condition, may be cleaned with a damp sponge or damp brush, or even soaked in water, but as a rule soaking should be avoided, as old ivory is very liable to split when wet. Ivory in poor condition should not be wetted.

5. Metals may generally be washed, but should always be thoroughly dried after-

wards. In the case of silver, copper and bronze that are corroded, washing is sometimes a useful preliminary to further treatment and is always necessary after treatment.

6. Gesso and plaster, unless gilt or varnished, should never be wetted.

7. Textile fabrics should not be wetted unless they are in good condition, in which case they may be soaked, if it is necessary to clean them or to remove salt.

8. Papyrus and paper will both stand a limited amount of soaking, but special precautions are necessary in handling them while wet.

9. Parchment and vellum should never be wetted.

If water cannot be used, or if it has been used without success, petroleum spirit should be tried. This is applied with a camel-hair or similar soft brush, and will be found useful for painted unvarnished surfaces, when the paint is not an oil-paint (for which it is unsuitable), and generally also for varnished surfaces. Petroleum spirit is useless unless an object is quite dry. In some cases, for example, on painted unvarnished surfaces, petroleum spirit may sometimes be replaced with advantage by alcohol, but alcohol should never be used on varnish, as resins, which are the basis of most varnishes, are soluble in alcohol. Alcohol, however, may be employed with safety on both unvarnished oil-paint and on waxed surfaces. The brush used, either with petroleum spirit or with alcohol, should be well rinsed in the liquid each time after having been applied to the object, and the liquid should frequently be renewed.

When water, petroleum spirit and alcohol all prove ineffectual, special treatment is necessary, the nature of which can only be known from the kind of material and the cause of any disfigurement, and no general rules are possible. A few hints, however, may be given. These are as follows:

1. Acids and alkalies should never be employed indiscriminately for the removal of deposits, incrustations and discolorations that resist the ordinary solvents and never without a certain knowledge that they will not injuriously affect the object treated, and when employed it should only be in the form of dilute solutions, every trace of which must afterwards be removed by thorough washing. The use of these reagents will be described when dealing with the various materials.

2. Attempts should not be made to scrape or chip off hard deposits or incrustations with a penknife or other instrument, though this is often done. Thus chloride of silver is sometimes chipped off silver objects and carbonate and sulphate of lime from ivory, pottery or stone. Chipping, however, except in the cases of copper, bronze and iron, is never satisfactory, and the object will almost certainly be disfigured by scratches or even more serious damage may result. The methods of treating various incrustations will be described when dealing with the materials on which they occur.

3. Deposits and stains of an organic nature (grease, oil, resin, tar) require organic solvents to remove them, and if petroleum spirit or alcohol are not effectual such solvents as acetone, benzol or pyridine should be tried.

Two very important cautions in connection with the cleaning of antique objects that must be observed if success is to be obtained are, firstly, that all cleaning processes take time, and often a considerable time, and to hurry them means impairing their efficiency, and secondly, that it is necessary to learn when " to let well alone," and not to try and push the cleaning process too far, otherwise damage will be done.

The next step in restoration after cleaning is repairing, and this therefore will now be considered.

Repairing By repairing or mending is meant the refixing of loose or broken pieces, and not the addition of new material, which will be considered later. Success in repairing is a matter of manipulative skill, training, experience, patience and care. Special training in repair work and the highest degree of manipulative skill will not fall to the lot of every one who is called upon to handle antique objects, but experience, patience and care may be acquired by all.

Repairs to antique objects are of such a varied nature that no detailed description is possible, and all that can be done is to give a few general principles, which are as follows :

1. Always well clean an object before repairing it.

2. Completely remove old cementing material before adding fresh. This should never be scraped off when dry, but must be softened first. Glue may be softened by means of warm water, beeswax with chloroform, resin with alcohol, and paraffin wax with petroleum spirit or by heat. The solvent used should be applied with a small

brush and the softened cement wiped off with a rag or removed by means of a piece of wood or bone, such as a small paper-knife.

3. Only the best quality cementing material should be employed.

4. Patent or secret preparations of cementing material should not be used unless their general nature is known and unless their value has been well proved.

5. The manner in which the various pieces of a broken object fit together should be ascertained by careful inspection and arrangement, but, as a rule, and especially if the material is friable or easily broken, the pieces should not be put actually touching one another before applying the cement, or the edges may break further.

Adhesives   Adhesives being essential to repairing may now be considered. They are of many different kinds, but the only ones that need be mentioned in this connection are glue, casein adhesive, celluloid cement, and plaster of Paris. These will now be described.

Glue.—Glue is an impure gelatin, generally extracted from animal bones, skins, cartilage or tendons, but also from fish. It is one of the oldest, best known, and most reliable of all adhesives, especially for wood. It was largely used by the ancient Egyptians, and in many instances glue on objects more than 3,000 years old is still in good condition.

Only the best quality glue and of as light a colour and as free from smell as possible should be employed. Glue, like every other soluble material, dissolves more quickly the finer the state of division, and therefore should be broken into small pieces before use. This is best done by wrapping it in several folds of cloth and breaking it with a hammer. The broken pieces should then be placed in the glue-pot and just covered with water and allowed to soak for several hours but not longer, or the surface will become covered with mould. The pot should then be placed in water which is boiled until the glue is thoroughly hot and liquid. An ordinary pottery (not glass) jam-jar makes an excellent glue-pot, but should be provided with a cover in order to diminish evaporation and so prevent the glue from thickening.

For use glue should be fairly thin, about the consistency of golden syrup, but not too thin or watery, and it should be used hot. Thick or tepid glue should never be employed.

Glue is best applied by means of a brush or stick. Two forms of both will be found useful, one flat and the other round and pointed; these should be in several sizes. The brush or stick should never be left in the glue after use, but should be removed and well washed in hot water. To mend a broken object the glue is evenly distributed as a thin film on both surfaces which, if possible, should be warmed first, and these are then pressed tightly together and clamped or tied with string until the glue has set, which will take at least several hours. The greater part of any glue that oozes out is wiped off at once with a rag, but no attempt should be made to clean the surface thoroughly until the joint has set, when any glue remaining may be removed with hot water and a soft rag.

To prevent the clamps from marking the object, the surface should be protected by thin pieces of board or cardboard. When string is used, pads of folded paper should be placed under the string at the edges. A wooden peg inserted in the string and twisted in the manner of a tourniquet will be found useful for tightening. For some purposes clothes-pegs of the kind provided with a spring, or trouser clips as used by cyclists, make useful clamps.

Casein Adhesive.—Casein is the protein from milk, and for the preparation of an adhesive this protein is precipitated by acids, washed, dried, ground and mixed with small proportions of other materials, such as carbonate of soda, fluoride of sodium and slaked lime.

Casein adhesive is frequently called " cold water glue," and is sold in the form of a fine powder, which only requires mixing with cold water to be ready for use. It is about equal to the best glue in adhesive properties.

Celluloid cement consists of celluloid dissolved in an appropriate solvent. A satisfactory cement may be prepared by dissolving celluloid in amyl acetate or in acetone or in a mixture of the two. The celluloid is rasped or cut into small fragments and put into a bottle, which is then nearly filled with the solvent chosen and repeatedly shaken and finally left overnight. Sufficient celluloid should be used to make a syrupy solution, which is ensured if some remains undissolved at the bottom of the bottle. For use a little of the solution is poured into a small dish or saucer, and is left exposed, preferably in a warm place, until sufficient of the solvent has evaporated to produce in the remainder the right consistency for use. A cement of this nature is now on the market put up in tubes ready for use.

Celluloid cement is waterproof, and is admirably adapted for repairing faience, glass, inlay, pottery and small stone objects, but may also be used for wood and most other materials, including even metals. It is best applied with a small camel-hair brush or a small piece of pointed wood and, as it does not set very quickly, sufficient time must be allowed for complete setting before the object is disturbed.

When using the cement on a porous object, such as faience or pottery, it should be allowed to soak well in before making the joint, or preferably, before applying the cement, the broken surfaces should be coated repeatedly with the celluloid solution as it exists before evaporation. For slightly porous or non-porous material like glass or metal, the two surfaces should be coated with the cement and fitted together, and any surplus cement, which oozes out, wiped off. The pieces are then pulled apart, allowed to dry, and a second coat of the cement applied and the join made again. When dry, excess cement is removed with a soft rag or soft brush dipped in amyl acetate or in acetone.

As it is rarely possible to clamp articles of faience, glass and pottery while the cement sets in the manner adopted for wood, other methods of keeping the broken surfaces together must be employed. Occasionally string or thread can be used, but as a rule the best way is to keep the joint in such a position until set that the weight of the material itself presses the edges together. This may be done by standing the object in sand, plasticine or adhesive wax. When sand is used this should be clean, fine quartz sand, free from stones and dust, and should be sifted and washed before use.

Plaster of Paris.—This is employed for repairing large pottery and stone objects. Only the best quality plaster should be used.

To mix plaster, take as much water in a basin as will give the required quantity of plaster, and into this scatter or shake rapidly and uniformly dry plaster in fine powder until all the water appears to be absorbed and no free water remains on the surface. Stir or beat the mixture with a spoon until smooth. Use quickly.

It adds to the life and durability of plaster of Paris to treat it repeatedly when dry with a dilute solution of celluloid or of cellulose acetate. This gives a slightly polished appearance to the surface, which is not unpleasing, and after treatment the plaster may even be cleaned with a damp sponge without damage.

Plaster of Paris may also be given a good surface by impregnating it when thoroughly dry with very hot paraffin wax or stearine, any excess of which is removed by the heated blade of a penknife. The surface is then polished with French chalk and a pad of cotton-wool. Stearine imparts to plaster the colour of old ivory.

Plaster of Paris is slightly soluble in water, and therefore should not be used to repair objects required to be washed or to hold water.

rengthening   Sometimes an article, as, for instance, a piece of ivory, a textile fabric, gilt or painted gesso or other object is intact inasmuch as there are no parts missing, but is in such a fragile and delicate condition that it cannot be handled without falling to pieces. In such a case the object manifestly must be strengthened if it is to continue to exist.

The only way to treat such objects is to impregnate them with some substance that will consolidate them, and this must be applied in a liquid form. One of the most valuable of such substances is melted paraffin wax, another is a solution of celluloid, and a third a solution of cellulose acetate.

Paraffin wax is used in the molten condition and, as a rule, very hot, and the object treated should be thoroughly dry and, if possible, previously warmed, in order that the wax may soak well in and not congeal on the surface, and the operation should be carried out in a warm place.

In order to ensure the wax being thoroughly hot, a comparatively large amount should be melted at one time, and the vessel must be one with a spout, from which the wax can be poured. A flat-bottomed copper kettle having a long spout, taking off from near the bottom, will be found satisfactory. Solder should not be used for any of the joints.

A fine spray of any sort is a mistake, as the wax cools very quickly and, instead of penetrating the object, congeals on the surface.

For small objects, immersing them momentarily in the melted wax and allowing them to drain is as a rule satisfactory, but the object should be warm before immersion, in order to avoid too sudden a change of temperature and must be free from blisters or other air spaces, otherwise the imprisoned air in expanding and escaping will cause damage. Another very satisfactory way of treating small objects is to apply the wax by means of a glass pipette, one about 10 c.c. capacity being a useful size. The pipette should be placed quite close to the surface of the object, and the wax, which must be very hot, should be allowed to run out as quickly as possible. The use of a pipette, although a little difficult at first, is soon learned, and with care there is no danger of drawing hot wax into the mouth.

If the temperature of the object and of the wax are satisfactory, the wax sinks well in without leaving any excess visible on the surface. If, however, excess wax is left, in hollows and corners, for instance, or as drops at the edges, as much of this as possible should be removed while still soft by means of a small ivory or bone paper-knife. The last trace may be made either to sink in or to run off by carefully warming the object, or by slowly moving over it, almost but not quite touching the surface, a red-hot spatula or similar instrument, or by means of petroleum spirit.

Paraffin wax is colourless, damp-proof and practically unchangeable. It may be used for beadwork, bone, gesso, horn, ivory and wood, the last-named, however, being considerably darkened in colour. It should not be forgotten that ordinary paraffin wax is not of definite composition, but is a mixture of various, though related, substances possessing different melting-points, which may range from about 32° C. (89·6° F.) to about 80° C. (176° F.) and, in consequence, it has not a sharp melting-point, but begins to soften at a temperature much below that at which it melts. Wax with a high melting-point, therefore, should be used, otherwise it will soften during the summer or in a hot climate.

Celluloid is employed in dilute solution in amyl acetate or in acetone, or in a mixture of the two, and cellulose acetate in dilute solution in acetone. These solutions are either sprayed on the object or applied with a small camel-hair brush. They are used for bone, ivory, painted surfaces and textile fabrics. A useful form of spray is an atomizer or spraying apparatus as used for the throat.

Renewing This is the addition of new material to replace parts of an object that are missing.

There is a great difference of opinion as to what extent renewals are permissible. There is no doubt, however, that, if done

at all, they should be done well and unostentatiously, and should be in complete harmony with the original and, whenever possible, of similar material and also that a detailed descriptive and photographic record of the exact condition of the object, before it was treated, should be made, and none of the old material that can be preserved should be destroyed.

Renewals are sometimes absolutely necessary, as an object may become so unstable and insecure that new strengthening material must be added if absolute ruin is to be prevented. Sometimes, however, when only a few fragments of an object remain, a model, which is frankly new, is preferable to a restoration of which very little is original and which may be misleading. The danger of adding new material is that at some time the object may be accepted or described as being entirely original and so may deceive. No general rules can be laid down, but each case should be considered on its own merits.

CHAPTER II

PRESERVATION

The cleaning, repairing and strengthening of antique objects all help towards their preservation, but this treatment, useful and necessary as it is, is not sufficient, and merely to treat an object and then to put it in a museum and expect it to remain unchanged is unreasonable, and in many cases the object would last longer if left buried in the tomb. The principal dangers to museums and other collections that require to be guarded against are light, moisture and other atmospheric influences, dust, insects, bacteria and fungi. These will now be separately considered.

Light The destructive effect of direct sunlight on colours is so well known that it is often customary in ordinary households to draw down the blinds of a room exposed to the sun in order to prevent the fading of curtains, carpets and wall-paper. Not only, however, does sunlight cause certain colours to fade,

24

but it also causes articles, such as textile fabrics, paper, papyrus and wood, to become discoloured and tender.

Diffused daylight is also injurious, though to a less extent than direct sunlight, and even artificial light is not without effect, darkness in most cases being the only complete protection. Since, however, museum exhibits cannot be kept in darkness, the practical remedies are to avoid direct sunlight and to minimize the effects of diffused daylight by the use of shutters or black blinds to the windows when the museum is not open to the public, and of yellow blinds when the museum is open, if the sun is on the windows, or the light very bright, or of yellow covers or curtains to special show-cases containing objects that are particularly susceptible to light, except when these are actually being used. Instead of blinds yellow glass might be employed, but the extra expense is not necessary if the precautions mentioned are taken. Blue- or violet-coloured material for either glass or blinds should be avoided, since the blue and violet rays of light are chemically the most active.

Moisture and other Atmospheric Influences Many of the influences destructive of antique objects cannot operate in the absence of moisture. Thus moisture is essential to the life of bacteria and fungi to the action of salt, to many chemical changes, and probably to the fading caused by light. Moisture is also injurious on account of its solvent action on various materials, more particularly when it contains, as it practically always does, carbon dioxide derived from the air, and still more if it contains, as may happen, sulphur acids from the burning of coal or coal gas. The exclusion of moisture-laden air therefore is essential. This can be done by proper attention to heating and ventilation and by the use of museum cases in which the air having access is filtered through a drying agent such as calcium chloride, or by the use of calcium chloride inside the cases. If a drying agent is employed it is necessary that it should be kept in suitable receptacles, and that it should be renewed frequently, otherwise more damage may be caused than by omitting it. For some objects, such as mummies, the atmosphere of the case should be as dry as possible, but for other objects an absolutely dry atmosphere, which however would be difficult to obtain, is not desirable, thus wood, when quite dry, contracts and cracks, and any plaster or paint on the surface breaks off.

Among injurious atmospheric influences may be mentioned too high a temperature and too great a range of temperature, and as equable a temperature as possible should be obtained.

Dust   Dust is objectionable, not so much on account of any direct damage it causes, although this may happen, but more especially because its presence necessitates constant handling of the objects in order to clean them. The remedy against dust is to use special dust-proof cases, of which several kinds are obtainable.

Insects   Organic materials of almost all kinds are liable to be attacked and even utterly destroyed by insects. These comprise clothes beetles, clothes moths, cockroaches, furniture beetles, silver fish and white ants, and they consume feathers, fur, hair, horn, ivory, leather, mummies, skins, wood, woollen goods, and many other materials.

There are two ways of combating insect pests, firstly, to prevent their access to the materials liable to be attacked, and secondly, to kill them should the articles, in spite of all precautions, be invaded.

The best preventive measures are well-fitting show-cases, frequent inspection, and periodical cleaning, and, for such articles as feathers, fur, hair, skins and woollen goods, the keeping of naphthalene (which is more effective than camphor) in the cases.

The best cure for materials that are already attacked is fumigation with carbon disulphide. This is a liquid which, on exposure to the air, evaporates, forming a gas which is a very effective insecticide. Hydrocyanic acid gas (prussic acid gas) and sulphur might also be employed, but the former is so very poisonous that its use, except by those accustomed to it, is not recommended, and fumigation by sulphur is somewhat difficult to carry out.

The simplest and most satisfactory method of using carbon disulphide is to leave the liquid, contained in suitable receptacles, exposed for about a week in the show-case in which are the articles to be treated, or to remove the articles to a special airtight case in which the fumigation is carried out. Liquid carbon disulphide is very inflammable and very volatile, and the vapour also is very inflammable, and when mixed with air in certain small proportions is also explosive ; it must therefore be used with necessary precautions, and fires, naked lights and smoking in the vicinity must be avoided. Carbon disulphide has a very objectionable smell, but this soon disappears from the objects treated.

If for any reason carbon disulphide cannot be employed, carbon tetrachloride, another volatile liquid but the vapour of which is not inflammable, may be used instead. This, however, is less efficient than carbon disulphide.

Other preventives and remedies against certain kinds of insects are to spray the material with (a) petroleum spirit, (b) a solution of mercuric chloride (corrosive sublimate) in alcohol, which is very poisonous, or (c) a solution of naphthalene in carbon tetrachloride. Arsenic compounds and copper compounds, which are excellent insecticides, cannot, as a rule, be used for antique objects, as they can only be employed in solution in water and water generally is to be avoided. This subject will be dealt with further when the separate materials are being considered.

Bacteria and Fungi   Among the agents of destruction that gain access to antique objects and damage or destroy them, are bacteria and certain vegetable growths such as lichens and fungi (moulds). Thus, for example, bacteria attack mummies, lichens disfigure stone and old window glass, also aiding disintegration, and fungi damage paper, plaster, textile fabrics and wood. These agents all need moisture and warmth for their development, and although warmth cannot be avoided, objects can with care be kept dry. The treatment of objects attacked will be described when the objects themselves are being considered.

Handling When dealing with antique objects it should not be forgotten that the human hands, even when clean, are always more or less moist and greasy, and that perspiration contains acid bodies and salt. In a hot country the effects of acid perspiration are very noticeable, and in the summer in Egypt, for example, blue litmus paper held in the fingers is reddened. Metal and other objects susceptible to the action of moisture, acids and grease should therefore be handled as little as possible, and the hands should be covered with white cotton gloves or with a cloth.

Preservative Coatings Although an object may have been cleaned and restored, it is, as already mentioned, constantly subject to agencies, such as atmospheric influences and contact with the hands, that tend to injure and destroy it. To protect objects from these influences, one among the many means adopted is to coat them with some preservative that is

impermeable to moisture and acid. In
everyday life a common preservative is
ordinary oil-paint or ordinary varnish, and
in museums linseed oil is sometimes used
to protect bronze and iron objects, and
occasionally ordinary varnish is used for
bones. All these substances, however, are
too crude and too disfiguring to be employed
on objects of art, and fortunately there are
excellent substitutes that are almost colourless. Among these, two stand out as much
superior to the rest, namely, one a solution
of celluloid in amyl acetate or in acetone
or in a mixture of amyl acetate and acetone,
and the other a solution of cellulose acetate
in acetone. Celluloid is not very soluble in
amyl acetate, though sufficiently so for most
purposes, and if a stronger solution is required
acetone or a mixture of amyl acetate and
acetone is used. Acetone, too, being more
volatile than amyl acetate, dries more quickly.
Neither celluloid nor cellulose acetate, however, are perfect, as they tend to become
very slightly acid with lapse of time, and
cellulose acetate may also give an opalescent
surface unless quite dry.

To make these solutions, the best quality
and the purest materials only should be
employed. The celluloid is rasped or cut

into small pieces and placed in a bottle, which is then almost filled with the solvent and well shaken from time to time. The celluloid will probably not all dissolve, but this does not matter and, as the solution is used, more of the solvent should be added. The cellulose acetate will already be in the form of powder, but as it generally contains moisture it should be well dried before use. It will be found that solutions of almost any consistency can be made, but none thicker than a thin syrup will be required. Such solutions will contain from about 1 per cent. to about 5 per cent. of the celluloid or cellulose acetate, they are colourless, and unless used too strong do not impart any gloss to the object treated. The film produced is tough, elastic, colourless, transparent, and not affected by moisture. Celluloid gives a slightly better result than cellulose acetate.

Other colourless varnishes that may be mentioned are (a) a solution of dammar resin, generally wrongly called "gum" dammar, in benzol or in petroleum spirit, (b) a solution of mastic resin in alcohol, and (c) a solution of bleached shellac in alcohol.

CHAPTER III

APPLICATION OF METHODS TO SPECIFIC MATERIALS

The application to specific materials of the methods already outlined will now be described, the materials being treated in alphabetical order.

Alabaster The name alabaster is applied to two very different materials, one sulphate of lime and the other carbonate of lime, one form of each being very similar in appearance. Which of these two substances has the prior claim to the name will not be discussed, but although the ancient Egyptians occasionally used sulphate of lime for making small objects, the term alabaster in Egyptology always means carbonate of lime, and it is this material that was employed for sarcophagi, statues, statuettes, vases, and other objects. Occasionally it is called " Oriental " alabaster, or sometimes " onyx marble," but both names are bad. Geologically the material is calcite, though sometimes erroneously termed aragonite, a material of similar composition, but different crystalline form and different specific gravity. Although aragonite may occur it is not common, and all the specimens of Egyptian alabaster examined by the author have been calcite.

The first step in the cleaning of alabaster is careful washing with good quality soap and warm water, aided if necessary by a small and not too hard a brush. All ordinary dirt and even most unpromising-looking stains may be removed in this way. After washing, the object should be well rinsed in clean water and placed on a clean cloth to drain and dry.

If there are stains that water will not remove, petroleum spirit, alcohol, acetone and benzol should be tried in the order named, that particular reagent being used that gives the best results.

If the object is a vase, it may contain decomposed organic matter, which unless removed may detract very much from the appearance, as the walls of vases are frequently sufficiently thin and translucent for a dark material to show through. As much of the contents as possible should be scraped out with a piece of wood and, unless the material is definitely of a fatty nature, the vessel should be filled with warm (not hot) water and left to soak, and afterwards washed out repeatedly with warm water. A piece of cloth tied to the end of a stick, or a brush, such as is used in chemical laboratories for cleaning bottles, will be found useful.

If the contents of a vase are of a fatty nature, or if water will not remove them, petroleum spirit, alcohol, acetone and benzol should be tried in the order named, the one which gives the best results being used. For petroleum spirit to be effective the material must be thoroughly dry, and therefore, if water has been used, this must be removed, and the best and quickest way of doing this is to rinse with alcohol, which takes up the water, drain and place in a warm place to dry, alcohol drying much quicker than water. Petroleum spirit is satisfactory for fatty matter, alcohol for resinous matter, and acetone and benzol for many miscellaneous materials of an organic nature. Considerable time and patience are frequently required to clean the inside of a vase.

Acids must never be employed to clean alabaster, as they act upon and dissolve it.

Occasionally, round the top of an alabaster vase, there may be the remains of cementing material used to fasten on a lid. This is frequently beeswax or resin, and it is generally brittle and the greater part may readily be removed with a penknife. It should not be forgotten, however, that alabaster is a fairly soft material, and is easily cut or scratched, and when it has been in contact with organic matter of an acid nature, such as decomposed fatty matter, it becomes very soft and friable. If a knife is used, therefore, great care must be taken to avoid injuring the surface of the alabaster, and no attempt should be made to remove the last traces of the cementing material in this way, as it is almost impossible to do so without damage, the final stages of the cleaning being done by means of a solvent, such as chloroform for beeswax and alcohol for resin. Other solvents, among which are acetone, petroleum spirit and hot alcohol, will also soften beeswax, but will not dissolve it, and might be used when chloroform is not obtainable. The solvent is applied with a rag or brush, and the cement when softened may be scraped off with a piece of bone or wood, such as a small paper-knife.

Alabaster may be repaired with celluloid

cement in the case of small articles or with plaster of Paris for large objects. Missing parts may be replaced by plaster of Paris, which when dry is treated with celluloid, cellulose acetate, paraffin wax or stearine, as already described.[1]

Since amber is a fossil resin any particular piece from a tomb had been buried for geological ages before it was found and used by man, and therefore burial for a few thousand years more does not usually affect it, and it is generally in good condition, though sometimes dirty. It is best cleaned by careful washing with good quality soap and warm water, aided by gentle rubbing with the fingers, followed by rinsing in clean water and drying.

Resins, other than amber, are often very brittle, and may be too tender to bear much treatment. Washing in warm water or cleaning with a damp camel-hair brush may however be tried, but should not be persisted in unless it is manifest that no harm is being done.

Organic solvents (alcohol, acetone, benzol) should on no account be employed for cleaning amber or other resins, as many of them soften and dissolve resin. This

[1] Pp. 19–22.

solvent action may be utilized if, as sometimes happens, the surfaces of resin beads or other objects are disintegrating and flaking off. In such cases the object should be sprayed repeatedly with alcohol or acetone, either of which will cause the loose surface to become sticky and to adhere again.

Amber and other resins may be repaired with celluloid cement, or in the case of resins other than amber (amber being too insoluble), by moistening the broken surfaces with alcohol or acetone and then pressing them tightly together.

In connection with resin, the black varnish-like coating on many wooden funerary objects from ancient Egypt, which is generally wrongly termed bitumen, pitch or tar, may be mentioned. This material is a naturally black resin of a lacquer-like nature, which often is not very adherent, but tends to flake off. It may be fixed and made to adhere again by spraying repeatedly with alcohol or acetone.

Baskets and Reed Work

Reeds, rushes and the stems of water-plants of various kinds, including papyrus, have been employed from very early times for making baskets, boxes, sandals and other objects. Such articles become very dry and brittle with lapse of time, but otherwise are generally in a fairly good state of preservation.

If the condition of the object will allow, superficial dust and dirt may be removed by gentle blowing with a small pair of bellows or careful brushing with a small soft brush. In the case of very fragile objects, the careful application of petroleum spirit with a small camel-hair brush will be found helpful for cleaning, and a brush thus moistened may often be used when a dry brush would cause damage. Water should not be used.

Objects of the kind under consideration may be strengthened and preserved by saturating them with melted paraffin wax. The material, being absorbent, takes the wax well, and if this is applied quickly and very hot no excess will be visible on the surface. The colour will be darkened somewhat, but the result is not unpleasing, and the object will be firm and will last indefinitely. Excess wax may be removed in the manner already described.[1]

Beads Beads are of so many different kinds and vary so much in the material of which they are made that no general directions for treatment can be given.

[1] P. 21.

As a rule all beads, with the exception of those of wood and of resin, will stand washing with soap and warm water. Gilt wooden beads, which occur occasionally, and resin beads, unless in bad condition, may be cleaned with a damp camel-hair brush.[1]

The holes in beads may be freed from dirt and old thread by means of a thin piece of wire for the larger and more solid beads and with a stiff bristle for smaller or more fragile ones. In cases in which the hole is solidly blocked up and the blocking material is very hard, great care is needed not to split the bead or not to chip the edges of the hole. Damage, however, may generally be avoided by well soaking the bead in water to soften and loosen the obstruction before using the wire or bristle.

Faience beads, with which may be included faience pendants for necklaces, often have not been well glazed originally, and the glaze may be decomposed with the formation of a whitish coating on the surface. All such objects should be well soaked in repeated changes of pure water until free from salt, and during soaking they should be removed from the water from time to

[1] See also " Amber and other Resins."

time and carefully brushed with a small brush.[1]

Great care is necessary in handling faience pendants, as the eyehole is easily damaged. When the projecting piece containing the eyehole breaks off this may be refastened in place with celluloid cement, but if the eyehole itself breaks the best remedy is to make a fresh one by cementing on a small bead of the requisite colour.

Beadwork when found is often in a fragile condition, owing to the material on which the beads have been sewn, or to the thread used, having perished. In such cases it may be consolidated by treatment with melted paraffin wax, as originally described by Flinders Petrie. If the wax is required to soak well in it should be applied very hot, but if much penetration is undesirable, as likely to cause the beads to adhere to objects below, the wax should be almost on the point of solidification before use. Excess wax may be removed as already described.[2]

Clay   Only unbaked clay will be considered, baked clay being dealt with as pottery. Clay objects include moulds, seals and inscribed tablets. As clay falls to pieces when wetted it cannot therefore be washed.

[1] See also " Faience."   [2] P. 21.

After removing superficial dust and dirt by blowing or brushing, clay objects should be hardened by baking. The fact that the appearance is altered somewhat and the colour changed should not be allowed to stand in the way of treatment, as the life of dried clay is very short and baking is the only satisfactory method of prolonging it. With a little experience or by means of preliminary experiments, aided by Seger cones or pyrometers, the best temperature and the necessary time for the baking can be found within narrow limits. Too great a temperature and too sudden a rise of temperature should be avoided. For small objects a gas or electric muffle furnace similar to those used in chemical laboratories will be found satisfactory.

After baking, clay objects if necessary may be soaked in water to remove salt or treated with dilute hydrochloric acid to remove concretions of carbonate of lime. If this be done, the objects must afterwards be soaked in repeated changes of water until on testing no trace of acid can be found. The object is then slowly but thoroughly dried. Any crystals of sulphate of lime on the surface will be dehydrated and fall to powder during baking.

Broken objects may be repaired (after
baking) either with celluloid cement or with
plaster of Paris suitably tinted. Missing
parts may be replaced by tinted plaster,
which is afterwards treated with celluloid,
cellulose acetate, paraffin wax or stearine,
as already described.[1]

Faience By faience is meant Egyptian faience.
This consists of a highly siliceous body
coated with glaze which is generally coloured
and is often blue or green.

The glaze of faience is particularly liable
to disintegration. Occasionally there is a
cracking and partial peeling of the whole
depth of the glazed surface, leaving bare
patches of the body exposed. This is caused
by a different rate of expansion and contraction between the glaze and the body. There
is no remedy, but fortunately it is not progressive, and patches only of the glaze fall
off. When the pieces of fallen glaze exist
they may be cemented in place again with
celluloid cement. As a rule it will be found
that the pieces are larger than the place
from which they have fallen, owing to the
body having contracted or the glaze having
expanded, but with care they may be
adjusted until they fit by means of a small

[1] Pp. 19–22.

fine file or with fine emery paper moistened with paraffin oil (kerosene).

Generally the decomposition of faience takes the form of a disintegration of the glaze accompanied by a white crystalline deposit on the surface. This deposit is ordinarily highly siliceous, but frequently contains also small proportions of carbonate of soda and common salt, with occasionally sulphate of soda. The carbonate of soda is formed from the alkali of the glaze and the carbon dioxide of the air, and any common salt or sulphate of soda present originate in the natron used for making the glaze, in which they occur as impurities. This disintegration is very unsightly, and results in the destruction of the surface and the disappearance of the colour. Sometimes, however, the colour disappears or changes without any signs of disintegration of the glaze; thus blue becomes green or fades to white and green turns brown.

The phenomena described are manifestly caused by some chemical decomposition having taken place in the glaze. The agents responsible are moisture and carbon dioxide. The mechanism of the action is probably much as follows. The glaze is porous and contains a large proportion of alkali; moisture containing carbon dioxide in solution condenses on the surface and is absorbed ; this decomposes the alkaline silicates, the result being a disintegration of the glaze with the deposition on the surface of the products of decomposition, sometimes in the form of a white or slightly tinted loose film, which eventually scales off or may be removed by brushing or scraping, but often as a white coating of which only a small part can be removed, the greater part consisting of strongly adherent crystalline siliceous material. Concurrently with this disintegration the material which gives the colour to the glaze may undergo chemical change and, as already stated, blue may become green or white and green may turn brown. Frequently, however, much of the colour is merely obscured and not destroyed.

Although the glaze of faience is essentially glass, it is much more subject to disintegration than glass, probably because it has been fused at a lower temperature and therefore is more porous, and, for the same reason, may contain common salt and sulphate of soda, both derived from the natron used in the manufacture and both of which would disappear at a higher temperature.

In addition to the disintegration described,

which is largely chemical and from within, although initiated and aided by outside influences, there is another form which may occur which is wholly physical and from without. This is confined to objects which have been in contact with salt and which have been alternately wet and dry. In this case the faience, which is very porous, becomes impregnated with a solution of salt, and when the object dries, the salt is brought to the surface by capillary attraction, and as the water holding it in solution evaporates, the salt crystallizes, and by the mere act of crystallization forces off particles of the glaze.

The best method of treating faience is as follows :

1. Wash well with warm water and soap, using a small sponge or soft brush. This removes superficial dirt.

2. Soak well in repeated changes of water until free from sulphate of soda and common salt. Gently boiling the water will help by the mechanical stirring set up, but boiling water has no great advantage over warm water as a solvent for common salt. When in the water the colour of the glaze will appear very bright, and any white surface deposit will be hardly visible.

3. Dry thoroughly but slowly, and at not too high a temperature. The result will be disappointing, since any white deposit, in so far as it consists of siliceous material, will now be apparent again and will obscure the colour of the glaze.

4. If there is still a white or tinted coating on the surface, brushing with a small hard brush or rubbing with very fine emery paper should be tried. Occasionally much of the film may be removed in this way, though more frequently the treatment is without effect. Rinse well in water and dry thoroughly.

5. Warm.

6. Rub over with a very small quantity of white vaseline, applied with a soft cloth or with the fingers, in such a manner that no excess vaseline remains on the surface. Although yellow vaseline is better than white vaseline for many purposes and is less liable to contain acid, yet the yellow variety should not be used in this instance, because if the glaze is coloured blue, as is frequently the case, the yellow of the vaseline would tend to give the blue a greenish tinge. The white deposit will become almost invisible and the original colour will once more be seen, as

was the case when the object was soaking in water. Olive-oil,[1] poppy seed oil [1] and melted paraffin wax [2] have all been recommended for a similar purpose, but vaseline is the most satisfactory.

The explanation of the action of the vaseline, oil, or wax is that the white appearance of the faience is due to the reflection of light from the irregular surfaces of the crystalline deposit, but when the air is removed and replaced by a substance, such as one of those mentioned, the refractive index of which is approximately that of the material itself, the crystals become almost transparent and the colour of the glaze underneath is seen through.

The use of acid, caustic soda, or carbonate of soda for cleaning faience is usually unnecessary and not to be recommended, partly because these reagents tend to act upon the glaze and to destroy it, and partly because they are very difficult to remove afterwards, even by repeated washing.

Broken faience is best repaired with celluloid cement. Missing parts may be replaced by plaster of Paris.

[1] *The Preservation of Antiquities.* F. Rathgen, Cambridge, 1905, p. 151.
[2] *Methods and Aims in Archæology.* F. Petrie, London, 1904, p. 89.

Feathers and Hair

Feathers become very tender and brittle with age, but may be strengthened by spraying with a very dilute solution of celluloid or of cellulose acetate. Care must be taken that the liquid is delivered in a very fine spray and that the feathers do not become saturated with the solution, otherwise the finer portions will stick together and the appearance will be spoiled. A spraying apparatus, such as is used for the throat, will be found satisfactory.

Hair is very resistant to ordinary influences of decay, and as a rule will not require treatment.

Both feathers and hair are very liable to be attacked by insects and should therefore be kept in cases that will exclude these pests; they should also be examined periodically, and naphthalene should be kept in the case. A further safeguard is to spray them with a solution of mercuric chloride (corrosive sublimate) in alcohol. If actually attacked by insects they should be fumigated with carbon disulphide in the manner already described.[1]

GESSO AND PLASTER

The terms "gesso" and "plaster" are used very loosely and are often applied

[1] P. 28.

indiscriminately to very different materials. The Egyptian materials will be taken as the types.

Gesso   Gesso was largely employed by the ancient Egyptians for covering wood before painting or gilding, and was applied either directly to the wood or to a layer of canvas-like material, which was glued to the wood. It is composed of whiting (carbonate of lime) and size or glue. Being a soft material, gesso is easily damaged mechanically ; it is also readily disintegrated by water, but is rarely subject to chemical alteration or decomposition on keeping or exposure. The great danger to which gesso is liable arises from alteration in volume of the wood to which it is attached, contraction or splitting of the wood, caused by drying, results in the gesso becoming loose or breaking off, especially at joints and corners.

Gesso, which is gilt, may be cleaned with a damp sponge or a small, soft, damp brush. A little soap dissolved in the water or a little ammonia added generally helps. If the gesso is cracked, or flaking off, or in bad condition, the minimum amount of water should be used, and care should be taken that none enters the cracks or penetrates under the gilt surface, or it will disintegrate the gesso. In very bad cases water should be avoided altogether and petroleum spirit used instead.

Gesso that is painted, but not varnished, may be cleaned either with petroleum spirit or alcohol, using a small soft brush, but not with water, as the paint would come off if wetted.

Gesso that is both painted and varnished may be cleaned with a damp sponge or a damp brush or with petroleum spirit but not with alcohol, as this might soften or dissolve the varnish. If water is used care should be taken that none enters any cracks that may be present or penetrates under the varnish, since, as already mentioned, this would cause disintegration of the gesso.

When gesso, which is gilt and varnished, or painted and varnished, is in good condition, no treatment beyond cleaning will be required, but when painted and not varnished, the paint, which rubs off readily, may be made to adhere again by spraying with a dilute solution of celluloid or of cellulose acetate.

Broken gesso may be repaired with celluloid cement. Gesso in a bad state of preservation should be consolidated by impregnation with melted paraffin wax. Before applying the wax the gesso should be warmed if possible, and the wax should be put on very hot. When properly applied the wax will all sink in and will hardly be apparent, but should any excess remain on the surface in a manner to cause disfigurement, this may be removed by heat, as already described.[1] Gilt and paint are both brightened by the wax.

Blisters in gesso should be filled with melted paraffin wax by means of a pipette and, just before the wax hardens, the blister should be pressed down firmly with the hands.

Plaster   By plaster is meant the various qualities of sulphate of lime ranging from crude gypsum to fine plaster of Paris. Plaster was employed in ancient Egypt for filling up holes and smoothing irregularities in stone, for coating walls before painting and for making moulds and casts.

Plaster, like gesso, is soluble in water, and therefore should never be wetted. Superficial dust and dirt may be removed by blowing or brushing, any further cleaning being done by means of petroleum spirit or alcohol and a soft brush. If painted, and if the paint shows signs of coming off, it should be sprayed with a dilute solution of celluloid or of cellulose acetate.

[1] P. 21.

Glass Glass is not the unalterable impermeable material generally supposed. This is
especially true of ancient glass, which
as a rule is softer, and was originally
softer, than modern glass, on account of
its containing a much larger proportion of
alkali.

The decomposition of glass is sometimes
not more than a slight dimming of the surface, but more generally small particles scale
off leaving the surface pitted, or the whole
surface may crack and scale. This latter
condition is often accompanied by an iri-
descence, which is purely an optical effect
produced by the breaking up of the white
light as it is reflected from the numberless
small colourless scales which result from the
decomposition. Occasionally glass may become so rotten that it falls to powder, but
fortunately this extreme form of disintegration is very rare.

Apart from the chemical decomposition
of the glass itself, the colour often undergoes
change. Thus white glass of ordinary quality
containing manganese compounds becomes
coloured when exposed for some time to
strong sunlight. This colour varies from a
very slight to a deep amethyst colour. In
Egypt it is a matter of common observation

to find on the desert, in the neighbourhood of towns, pieces of what has been white glass coloured in this manner. The depth of colour appears to vary with the time of exposure. Other colour changes may also occur in glass, for example, the blue colour of old Egyptian glass, when this is due to copper and not to cobalt, sometimes changes to green and the colours of stained-glass windows undergo slight changes of tint as the result of long exposure, which generally mellow them and add to their beauty.

The decomposition of glass is due, in the first place, to the fact that the glass contains an excess of alkali, and in the second place, to the further fact that glass is hygroscopic and condenses on its surface moisture from the atmosphere, containing carbon dioxide in solution. The result is a chemical decomposition with the formation of carbonate of soda and the separation of silicate of lime and probably some silica.

The only cure for glass that is disintegrating is to soak it in repeated changes of warm water until free from all soluble salts and free caustic or carbonated alkali, allow it to drain, soak in alcohol, dry thoroughly, and then coat it with a transparent varnish, such as a solution of celluloid or of cellulose acetate. Any necessary repairs may be made with celluloid cement.

The old Egyptian red glass, which is coloured with copper, is liable to surface decomposition, with the result that it becomes covered with a green coating. This is very resistant to treatment, but may generally be removed by boiling in strong caustic soda solution followed by thorough washing in water until all traces of the soda are removed. The surface, however, will be left deeply pitted.

IVORY, BONE AND HORN

Ivory The condition of ivory objects as found varies considerably, some being in a very good state of preservation, while others are so brittle as to make even handling difficult, and many ivory objects from Egypt, in consequence of containing salt, are particularly delicate.

When in good condition, ivory may be cleaned by means of a damp sponge or damp brush, but it should not be wetted much as it is very liable to split into flakes. Occasionally, however, ivory, and even the most ancient ivory, may be soaked in water without damage, and this treatment is often

very desirable in order to remove salt, but
it cannot be adopted as a routine practice,
owing to the uncertainty of the results.
Although the appearance and condition of
an object are some guide to its probable
behaviour in water, it is generally impossible
to be certain beforehand that a particular
piece of ivory will stand soaking, and the
safe rule, therefore, is to avoid water. In the
exceptional case in which the risk is taken
and an ivory object is soaked, this should
first be done in ordinary pure water and afterwards in distilled water, followed by alcohol
and slow drying without artificial heat.

After cleaning, ivory may be strengthened
by spraying or brushing with a solution of
celluloid or of cellulose acetate. Even using
a dilute solution a slight glaze may be produced, but this is not objectionable, and gives
the effect of the polish usually seen on ivory
objects, but much glaze should be avoided.
Excess glaze may be removed by means of
amyl acetate or acetone applied on a tuft
of cotton-wool.

For ivory in bad condition there is only
one remedy, namely, impregnation with
celluloid, cellulose acetate or melted paraffin
wax, and this must be done without any
attempt being made to remove any salt

present. Before treatment the object should be cleaned as well as possible by gentle blowing and brushing, followed by further brushing with a small soft brush damped with alcohol. Sometimes the alcohol will loosen adherent earthy matter, which may be removed. The object is then slowly dried and, if celluloid or cellulose acetate are used, these are applied either with a small camel-hair brush or in the form of a spray. If wax is employed, the object, previously warmed, if possible, is placed on supports in order that it may drain, and treated, first on one side and then on the other, with hot melted paraffin wax. The wax should be applied quickly in a thin stream, which is best done by means of a pipette. If the temperature of the object and of the wax are satisfactory the wax sinks well in without leaving any excess visible on the surface. If, however, excess wax is left, this may be removed in the manner already described.[1] One objection, though not a serious one, to the use of paraffin wax is that it may slightly darken the ivory.

Not infrequently ivory objects found in Egypt are coated with a hard incrustation of carbonate of lime, or of sand and earth

[1] P. 21.

bound together by carbonate of lime. This
can only be removed by acid, hydrochloric
acid being the best. The acid should be
very dilute (about 1 to 2 per cent.), and is
best applied by brushing it repeatedly over
the incrustation with a camel-hair brush.
After treatment it is essential that every
trace of acid should be washed out by soaking the object in repeated changes of water,
until on testing the washings are found to
be acid free. It is only ivory in an excep-
tionally good state of preservation that will
stand such treatment.

Ivory objects may be repaired with celluloid cement.

Bone   Bones and bone objects may generally be
cleaned by washing with soap and warm
water. If salt is present this may be removed
by soaking in repeated changes of water
until it is all dissolved out, which may be
ascertained by testing. The object should
be dried slowly. If the bone is cracked, or
is not in good condition, it may be wrapped
tightly in gauze or tied round with fine
string before soaking.

For repairing small bone objects, celluloid
cement may be used, and for large objects
glue or plaster of Paris. After cleaning and
repairing, bones and bone objects should

be brushed over with a solution of celluloid or of cellulose acetate. The practice sometimes employed of coating bones with ordinary painters' varnish should never be followed, as it can only result in discoloration and disfigurement.

Bones and bone objects in a fragile condition should be treated with celluloid, cellulose acetate or melted paraffin wax in the manner described for ivory.

Horn   As a rule horn requires little or no treatment beyond cleaning, which may generally be done with warm water. Horn, however, is subject to the attacks of insects, and even ivory and bone are not exempt, though less liable than horn to be attacked. The best preventive, and also the best remedy if the object is already attacked, is to spray or paint it with a solution of mercuric chloride in alcohol. This solution is very poisonous and must be used with care. Horn, if broken, is best repaired with celluloid cement or glue.

JEWELLERY AND ENAMEL

Jewellery   Ancient jewellery is generally made of gold or silver, or of these metals inlaid with stones, faience or glass.

Gold or silver articles, when not inlaid,

should be treated as described later when dealing with metals.

For inlay, whether with precious stones, semi-precious stones, faience or glass, soaking and washing in warm water, aided by a little good quality soap, together with gentle rubbing with a soft brush or soft cloth, will generally be sufficient. Sometimes faience and glass inlay has a coating on the surface which may be either a product of the decomposition of the material or may be largely the glue used as a cement which has come from the under side of the inlay. In the former case very little can be done beyond washing with water and when dry coating with a thin film of some transparent varnish, such as a solution of celluloid or of cellulose acetate. In the latter case the deposit can generally be removed by means of repeated applications of warm water, aided by gentle scraping.

One of the guiding principles in the cleaning of inlaid jewellery is to ascertain, if possible, the nature of the cementing material holding the inlay in place, and not to use any reagent that will soften or dissolve it. For example, if the cement consists of resin or contains resin, as is often the case, alcohol should not be used for cleaning ; if the cement contains whiting or gypsum, prolonged soaking in water must be avoided.

Acids and alkalies should never be used, for not only may the cement be dissolved, but some of the materials forming the inlay may be attacked, thus lapis lazuli, malachite and calcite are all acted upon by acids and turquoise is affected by alkalies.

To repair jewellery, when the inlay has come loose or fallen out, celluloid cement is recommended.

Enamel   Enamel is a vitreous material fused by heat on to a metal base, the difference between enamel and inlay being that the former is never a natural stone, but always a kind of glass (paste) fused in position, while the latter, which may consist of a variety of materials, is cemented in and never fused.

Enamel may be cleaned with a little warm water and soap and a soft brush.

For enamel that has cracked and is separating from the metal base, Dr. Alexander Scott [1] recommends treatment with a solution of Canada balsam in benzol, after partial exhaustion of the air, so that the balsam may penetrate well. This treatment has been adversely criticized on the

[1] *The Cleaning and Restoration of Museum Exhibits,* Dept. of Sci. and Ind. Research, London, 1921.

grounds that the balsam will darken in colour and will eventually crack and break up.[1] It is doubtful, however, whether any better method can be found.

Leather Leather is very subject to deterioration. It readily dries and becomes brittle, and there is evidence that occasionally when exposed for long periods of time to a moist heat in a closed tomb it becomes viscous and "runs," although when found it may be hard, brittle and lustrous, and very like pitch in general appearance. When in this condition it is softened by, and largely soluble in, water (as much as 85 per cent. being soluble in one specimen tested), and may be removed from objects to which it is adhering by means of hot water. It is, however, beyond treatment.

To keep leather in good condition, and to restore to some extent any suppleness it may have lost, oil or grease should be employed, but these are only of use if the deterioration has not proceeded too far. Any oil that readily becomes acid, such, for example, as neat's-foot oil and olive-oil, which are sometimes recommended, should be avoided, but castor oil, lanoline, sperm oil and vaseline may all be used. The oil or

[1] *J. Royal Society of Arts*, March 24, 1922, p. 336.

grease chosen should be warmed before use and should be smeared on the leather and well rubbed in, if the condition of this will allow, the treatment being repeated from time to time. When the leather is too brittle to bear much handling, the object may be soaked in the oil or the latter may be applied with a soft brush. The author has found a solution of lanoline in petroleum spirit, which may be sprayed on, sometimes gives good results.

Leather is subject to the attacks of various insects, particularly cockroaches and silver fish. These may easily be kept at bay by well-fitting show-cases, by frequent moving and dusting of the objects, and by spraying with a solution of mercuric chloride in alcohol, which is very poisonous and must be used with care.

METALS

The metals which will be dealt with are gold, silver, copper, bronze, iron, and lead.

Gold When gold is very pure it is a bright yellow colour and does not corrode or even tarnish and therefore requires no cleaning beyond the removal of dirt, which may be done by means of soap and warm water, aided by a soft cloth or small brush. The brush should not be hard, or it may scratch the gold, pure gold being soft and easily scratched. If there is any red patina on the gold, rubbing or brushing should be done with care, otherwise this patina, which is not only evidence of age, but also adds to the beauty of the object, may be destroyed.

Gold, however, is rarely pure, but generally contains small proportions of other metals, chiefly silver, copper and iron, which undergo chemical change and give rise to a surface discoloration or tarnish.

To clean gold when tarnished, it should first be washed with soap and warm water, with gentle rubbing with a soft cloth or brushing with a soft brush, and then treated with ammonia solution (10 per cent.), which is applied with a rag or camel-hair or similar brush. In the rare cases in which ammonia is not successful, cyanide of potassium should be tried, as this will remove tarnish due to sulphide of silver and sulphide of copper, which are not soluble in ammonia. This reagent should only be employed in very dilute solution (5 per cent.), as it acts upon and dissolves gold when used too strong or if left in contact with the gold too long. After treatment the object must be thoroughly washed in water and carefully dried.

Occasionally on the surface of gold there are patches of reddish-brown discoloration caused by organic matter. This is not soluble either in ammonia or in cyanide of potassium, but can usually be removed by the careful use of plate powder, such as whiting or jewellers' rouge, or by heating, if the nature of the object will permit.

Sometimes on ancient Egyptian gold objects there are incrustations of carbonate and sulphate of lime. No attempt should be made to scrape these off, as this would scratch and disfigure the gold, but any such deposits may be completely removed by soaking the object in a dilute solution of hydrochloric acid, which is without action on gold. The acid must be followed by thorough washing in pure water and drying.

A number of objects in the Cairo museum, which at first were thought to be of solid gold, were much defaced by incrustations, which appeared to be metallic, but which on chemical analysis were found to consist of chloride of silver in the form of " horn silver." It was further found that the objects were not of solid gold, but originally had been of silver coated with thin sheet gold, and the silver had become partly, and probably largely, converted into chloride, and it was from this that the incrustations had been derived. As ammonia is one of the best solvents for chloride of silver and could not injure the gold, the objects were soaked for several days in strong ammonia. The chloride of silver on the surface was entirely removed, that in the interior, being protected by the gold, was not noticeably attacked and the objects were left in excellent condition.

Gilt objects are cleaned in the same manner as those of solid gold or sheet gold, but when the gilt is thin, great care is needed to avoid damaging the surface and the cleaning should be done with a small soft brush. As old Egyptian gilt is generally on gesso, the precautions mentioned when dealing with this material [1] should be observed. Sometimes on the surface of gilt there is a characteristic reddish-brown deposit, which is confined to the vicinity of cracks and broken edges. This is largely an exudation of glue from underneath, and it may be removed by frequent applications of warm water used with a small piece of sponge or a soft brush.

[1] P. 50.

Silver   Silver as employed for making jewellery, ornaments, plate and other objects is never pure, but always contains other metals, notably copper.

Antique silver, and particularly old Egyptian silver, varies very much in its state of preservation, the severity of any corrosion ranging from a slight surface discoloration or tarnish to a condition so bad that the metal has wholly disappeared and has been replaced by the compounds resulting from the chemical changes that have taken place. Naturally these different conditions require different methods of treatment. As it is impossible to describe separately each of the infinite stages or degrees of corrosion, these will be divided for the sake of convenience into three main groups, namely, (a) tarnish, (b) slight corrosion, and (c) considerable corrosion. These will now be considered.

Tarnish.—This is a very thin, grey or black film on the surface of an object, which otherwise is in excellent condition and perfectly sound. On ancient objects the film ordinarily consists of chloride of silver, but occasionally may be sulphide of silver, together with a little sulphide of copper, or a mixture of chloride and sulphide. On modern silver, or on ancient silver that has acquired a recent tarnish, the film is usually sulphide.

The chloride has been caused by the action of a slight amount of common salt, such as might be present in the atmosphere, thus, for example, in Egypt salt occurs almost everywhere, in the limestone rock in which so many tombs are made and in the desert sand, and hence its presence in the dust in the air is not surprising. Salt also occurs in the air near the sea-coast. Sulphide that has been acquired anciently has come from contact with decaying organic matter containing sulphur and modern sulphide from exposure to an atmosphere contaminated with sulphur compounds derived from the burning of coal or coal gas.

A surface discoloration of the kind described may readily be removed, chloride of silver being soluble in ammonium hydrate (ammonia solution) and also in cyanide of potassium, and both sulphide of silver and sulphide of copper being soluble in cyanide of potassium.

Since the tarnish on ancient silver is commonly due to chloride and rarely to sulphide, ammonia therefore will generally remove it and, as ammonia is more easily procurable and less dangerous than cyanide of potassium, which is very poisonous, ammonia is to be preferred, a solution containing about 10 parts of strong ammonia to 100 parts of water being used. Ammonia, too, has the advantage of being almost without action on silver, and although it acts upon any copper present in the alloy this action under the conditions in which it is used is negligible. In the rare cases in which the tarnish is due to sulphide, cyanide of potassium (5 per cent. solution) must be used. This acts slightly upon silver, but if employed in dilute solution, and if the object is well washed afterwards this action may be disregarded. The ammonia, or cyanide, is best applied by means of a tuft of cotton-wool or with a small soft rag. After cleaning, the object must be thoroughly washed with pure water and carefully dried.

Slight Corrosion.—This, though largely consisting of chloride of silver, also contains compounds of copper originating in the copper alloyed with the silver. When the silver is of poor quality and contains a large proportion of copper the corrosion may be of a green colour, though this is unusual. As already stated, two excellent solvents for chloride of silver are ammonium hydrate (ammonia solution) and cyanide of potassium,

and these have already been recommended
for use in removing tarnish. But with any
corrosion greater than tarnish, simple rubbing the surface of the object with a dilute
solution of the solvent would be useless, and
it becomes necessary to soak the object in
the solution and to leave it for several hours
at least and possibly for days. Under these
conditions the use of cyanide of potassium
is not advisable, for not only does it attack
and dissolve silver to a slight extent, but
it also dissolves the gold of any gilding that
may be, and often is, present on silver
objects of certain kinds and periods.

Ammonia solution is almost without
action on metallic silver under ordinary
conditions, and if the silver of which objects
of art are made were pure, treatment with
ammonia would be an invaluable remedy
for corrosion, but the metal is not pure silver
but essentially an alloy of silver and copper,
and unfortunately ammonia attacks and
dissolves copper, even when alloyed with
other metals, and the action, though only
slight with alloys containing less than about
20 per cent. of copper, is considerable in
the case of alloys containing a larger proportion of copper. Since it is impossible
as a rule to know the composition of the

alloy operated upon, the use of ammonia
as a routine practice cannot be recommended,
though it is an exceedingly valuable reagent
that should not be neglected in the case of
high-quality silver that has become corroded.
To avoid the solvent action of ammonia this
may be mixed with ammonium sulphite or
sodium sulphite, as recommended by Dr.
Alexander Scott,[1] both of which compounds
are reducing agents and act upon the chloride
of silver, converting it back again into the
metallic state. A very small proportion of
either copper sulphite (cuprous) or copper
sulphate may be added, as without a copper
compound the whole of the chloride of silver
is not reduced. There may be, however,
sufficient copper present from the corrosion.
The object is immersed in the solution, which
is then heated.

One of the best reagents for the removal
of slight corrosion from silver is hot formic
acid, recommended by Dr. Alexander Scott.[2]
The object is placed in a glass, glazed
earthenware, or enamelled-iron vessel, metal
being avoided. A solution of formic acid
in water, sufficient to well cover the object,

[1] *The Cleaning and Restoration of Museum
Exhibits*, Dept. of Sci. and Ind. Research, London,
1921.   [2] *Ibid.*, 1921 and 1923.

is added and the solution heated. The
strength of the acid may vary from 5 to 25
per cent., but it is usually better to begin
with about 10 per cent. The object is
allowed to remain for several hours, when
it is taken out and examined. If the action
is not complete the object is replaced, the
strength of the acid being increased if necessary. The acid decomposes the copper
compounds present and also a portion of
the chloride of silver, with the result that,
although the whole of the corrosion may not
be decomposed, what is left is rendered less
adherent and generally either falls off or
may be brushed off while wet with a small
soft brush. The acid has no solvent action
on the silver. After treatment the object
must be thoroughly washed and carefully
dried. Formic acid is particularly valuable
for the treatment of objects made of poor
quality silver.

Considerable Corrosion.—Corrosion may be
so considerable that the object is coated
with a thick lumpy crust, which hides all
detail, not only of design, but also of shape,
the general outline of the object only being
recognizable, and it is sometimes impossible
to know what the object is. Occasionally
there may be a core of solid coherent silver

under the corrosion, but more often any silver remaining is in a very brittle and rotten condition, and frequently there is little or no silver left. This crust, like that on less corroded objects, consists largely of chloride of silver mixed with small proportions of copper compounds derived from the copper contained originally in the silver. Sometimes the chloride of silver is in the form of "horn silver," which is very adherent and which resembles lead somewhat both in appearance and hardness and which may be cut with a knife, but no attempt should be made to remove it in this manner, as the result would certainly be failure and probably disaster. When the object has a core of silver left, whether this is solid and coherent or not, it may be treated as already described for slight corrosion, namely, either with hot formic acid or with ammonium sulphite and ammonia or sodium sulphite and ammonia, but more prolonged treatment is necessary than in the case of slight corrosion. It is generally better, however, to commence by soaking the object in ammonia, a solution containing about 50 parts of strong ammonia to 100 parts of water being used, and to follow this by treatment with hot formic acid. Much of the corroded material will either dissolve or will fall off in the solutions, and the remainder may usually be detached while wet by gentle picking with a small bone or ivory paper-knife or similar instrument having a thin edge, or may be brushed off. After experience of the mechanical treatment of copper and bronze objects there will be a great temptation to attempt to flake a silver object in the same manner, but this must not on any account be done, as it is never safe, and no force whatever must be employed, otherwise damage will certainly result. After treatment, the object should be well washed in pure water and thoroughly dried.

If the silver under the corroded surface is in a coherent solid state the result of treatment will generally be satisfactory, and even if the silver core is brittle and rotten a satisfactory result may also be obtained, if care is taken in handling the object during treatment and particularly if no force is employed in removing any chloride left after treatment. Unless, however, great care is exercised the object will certainly break, as the silver has very little strength or cohesion. Occasionally the corrosion proves very obstinate, part only being removed, and in such cases a satisfactory result may be impossible and an improvement of the original condition all that can be obtained.

If an object, of which the walls were originally thin, is much corroded, it is certain that little or no metallic silver is left, and in such a case it is almost inevitable that during treatment the object will break or may even fall to pieces. This possibility, therefore, must be faced, and a decision made whether it is better to leave the object untouched and corroded, with sometimes its very nature unknown, or to risk damage and even total loss, in the hope that something of interest, or beauty, or even of archæological value, such as an inscription, may be saved. If it is decided to risk treatment, every care possible must be taken in handling the object, especially in the final stages. With objects in this tender condition no attempt should be made to remove loosened corrosion except with a camel-hair or similar soft brush.

Hollow objects such as boxes, vases and bowls that are very thin and tender may be strengthened by being lined or filled with paraffin wax. This is best applied by means of a pipette, and should be on the point of solidification when used. If there are holes in the object, through which the wax would run out, these should be stopped up from the outside with a thick coating of wax by means of a penknife, the wax being in the plastic condition that is found on the surface of a mass that is cooling. After the wax core is finished, the surplus wax on the outside may readily be removed with a penknife, the blade of which is heated in the flame of a bunsen lamp or spirit lamp. One great advantage of lining or filling an object with wax is the ease with which repairs may be executed. All that is necessary, if the loose piece is small, is to place it on the wax and touch it with the heated blade of a penknife, when it sinks into position. If the loose piece is large, it is placed in position before the lining or filling is done, and is held in place by plastering over the join from the outside with plastic wax, then applying a thick lining of wax inside and finally removing the excess wax from the outside with the heated blade of a penknife.

For small repairs to silver objects celluloid cement will be found satisfactory, and, if the silver is not very coherent, coating it with celluloid solution will strengthen and preserve it, the silver sometimes absorbing a large amount of the solution.

Copper and Bronze   The most important metal used in antiquity was copper, which at first was employed alone and afterwards in the form of bronze. This copper is never pure, but contains small proportions of other ingredients, the most common of which are antimony, arsenic, bismuth, iron, tin and sulphur. The total impurities generally amount to about 2 to 3 per cent., though sometimes they are more.

Bronze is essentially an alloy of copper and tin, with occasionally a little zinc. The proportion of the two metals in modern bronze is usually about 90 per cent. of copper to about 10 per cent. of tin. In ancient bronze the proportion of tin is not so constant as in the modern article, and varies from about 5 per cent. to about 16 per cent., but frequently it is about the same as in modern bronze, namely, about 10 per cent. The impurities in ancient copper are naturally found also in ancient bronze, with sometimes the addition of lead, which may be present in proportions ranging from a trace to about 20 per cent. The advantage of bronze over copper is twofold : firstly, it is harder than copper, and secondly, the melting-point is lower, thus enabling castings to be made more easily.

Copper and bronze objects corrode very

readily, the compounds formed being basic copper carbonates,[1] which may be either green or blue in colour, copper oxides, of which there are two, one red and the other black, and in Egypt generally copper oxychloride (green), due to the action of salt.

Cleaning of Copper and Bronze   Various methods of cleaning are in common use which are not satisfactory and are not recommended. These include the use of (*a*) ammonia, (*b*) hydrochloric acid, and (*c*) sulphuric acid.

Ammonia.—Ammonia should never be employed, as its action is not limited to the corrosion, but extends to the metal itself, which it also attacks. The results, too, especially on badly corroded objects, are not satisfactory.

Hydrochloric Acid.—Although hydrochloric acid has only a slight action on the metal, it also is not satisfactory, one great objection to its use being the difficulty of eliminating all traces of it afterwards. This acid, too, produces on the object treated a white coating of cuprous chloride, which is difficult to remove.

Sulphuric Acid.—Like hydrochloric acid, this acid has very little action on the metal if

[1] Often wrongly termed " verdigris," which is basic acetate.

used cold and dilute, but the results obtained with it are not satisfactory, and it is an unpleasant and dangerous substance to handle.

Ammonium Chloride.—Ammonium chloride, both alone and mixed with small proportions of stannous chloride and hydrochloric acid, has been suggested by Dr. Alexander Scott.[1] Alone, ammonium chloride has a slight action on copper and bronze, and the results of its use are not very satisfactory, the object often acquiring a white or unpleasant grey colour, which is difficult to remove and, if much corroded, being only imperfectly cleaned. The yellow coating sometimes formed, and which consists of cuprous oxide in the colloidal form, is readily brushed off. When the ammonium chloride is mixed with small proportions of stannous chloride and hydrochloric acid, the action on the metal is diminished and the results are much better, though frequently not so satisfactory as those obtained by means of an alkaline solution of Rochelle salt, also suggested by Dr. Scott,[1] and which, in the author's opinion, is the best all-round method for general use. Other methods recom-

[1] *The Cleaning and Restoration of Museum Exhibits,* Dept. of Sci. and Ind. Research, London, 1921 and 1923.

mended, besides Rochelle salt, are treatment
with acetic acid, reduction methods and mechanical methods.   These will now be described.

Rochelle Salt.—The Rochelle salt method
is carried out as follows : an alkaline solution of Rochelle salt (sodium potassium tar-
trate) is made containing 15 parts of Rochelle
salt and 5 parts of caustic soda to every 100
parts of water. The object is immersed
in this solution and left for some hours or
for a day or two, as is found necessary, being
taken out from time to time, rinsed in water
and well rubbed with the fingers or brushed
while wet with a small stiff brush, such as
a tooth-brush or nail-brush, or even with a
fine brass (not steel) wire brush, if after
trial this is found not to scratch the metal.
The small compound bristle and brass-wire
brush sold for cleaning brown shoes will be
found useful. On removal from the solution the object will usually be found coated
with a layer of red oxide which, unless very
thick, will be removed, or largely removed,
by the brushing, which may be supplemented
if necessary by the mechanical treatment
described later. The treatment of the object
should usually be finished in a bath of fresh
solution, the old solution being filtered and
put on one side to be used as the first bath

of another object. After cleaning, the object must be thoroughly washed in repeated changes of pure water and carefully dried. The results are very satisfactory, even for badly corroded objects.

Acetic Acid.—Acetic acid when dilute has very little action on copper or bronze, it removes corrosion well, is easily obtainable, and is not objectionable to use. The object is immersed in a dilute solution of the acid (about 10 parts of the strong acid to each 100 parts of water) and is left for some hours and if necessary for several days, until all the green corrosion has disappeared, and only a coating of red oxide is left. It is then taken out, well brushed as previously described, and if necessary subjected to the mechanical treatment dealt with later. It is finally repeatedly washed until free from all traces of acid and well dried. Formic acid is still more satisfactory than acetic acid, but its cost is considerably greater.

Reduction.—The methods of reduction depend upon the production of nascent hydrogen by the action of certain acids or alkalies upon certain metals. There are many variants, but acids should always be avoided if possible, as they may attack the metal itself and are always difficult to

G

eliminate afterwards. The simplest and best method is to employ zinc and caustic soda. The details of the process are as follows : take an iron saucepan or a porcelain basin and in this place a layer of granulated zinc. On the zinc lay the object to be treated and on this more zinc until the object is completely covered. Add a dilute solution (10 per cent.) of caustic soda, heat and allow to simmer gently for several hours. When the object is removed it will be found coated with a black deposit. It is rinsed in water and well brushed while still wet with a brass-wire brush. If the action appears incomplete the object is replaced and the boiling continued for a further length of time. Finally the object is thoroughly washed and well dried. The results of this treatment, although appearing satisfactory at the time, are often disappointing, as spots of green corrosion are very liable to appear later. When this happens, the spots are well brushed with a brass-wire brush and the treatment is repeated, or, better, the object is treated with Rochelle salt as already described.

Mechanical Treatment.—This is occasionally sufficient by itself, but more generally it will be found a useful auxiliary to the chemical treatment, and may be used either before or after or both, according to the nature of the corrosion. It is best applied when the object is wet, either after merely rinsing with water when it is removed from the solution in which it has been treated or after well wetting it with water. If the object is dry the fine dust created is very objectionable and is also injurious to the lungs.

The method consists in flaking off the corroded surface with a very small chisel of the kind used by jewellers, or with a watchmaker's hammer or even with a penknife. Sometimes almost the whole of a corroded surface will flake off leaving the metal clean and free from corrosion. The layer of red oxide of copper generally left after the Rochelle salt or acetic acid treatment may be rubbed or brushed off if thin, but if thick requires flaking off, when it readily comes away. As a rule mechanical treatment can only be applied to solid objects and not to those that are hollow or in a tender condition. After mechanical treatment it is usually better to treat the object with Rochelle salt.

Preservative Coatings.—Copper and bronze objects after being cleaned are frequently oiled or waxed. This spoils the appearance and is unnecessary, as a colourless varnish, of which several kinds are available, gives all the protection afforded by oil or wax and has the advantage of being scarcely visible. The best of these varnishes for copper and bronze is a dilute solution of celluloid or of cellulose acetate. If as the result of treatment a copper or bronze object is too bright, it is best left exposed to the atmosphere of an ordinary room for a time, when it becomes slightly tarnished, but if something more than this is required it may be given a black colour by immersing it in a dilute solution of sodium sulphide, after which it is rinsed in water and dried. The exposure to the air or the treatment with sodium sulphide must be done before varnishing, and before using either sodium sulphide or varnish the object must be freed from grease, which may be done by cleaning it with petroleum spirit. With respect to patina in general it is only necessary to inspect any exhibition of modern sculpture or the excellent reproductions of antique bronzes made in Italy and Greece, to realize that a copper or bronze object may be given almost any kind of patina desired. It should not be forgotten, however, that such patina is a surface corrosion which unless care is taken may gradually increase.

A useful book on the subject is mentioned in the Bibliography, but the methods given in the ordinary household book of recipes should generally be avoided.

Bacteria.—Statements are sometimes made that the corrosion of bronze in certain cases is caused by bacteria. This has never been proved and is most improbable, and all the observed facts in connection with such corrosion may be explained chemically.

Iron The fact that iron corrodes readily is a matter of common experience, and rusty iron may be seen almost everywhere. It is very noticeable, too, that on the sea-coast iron corrodes more quickly than inland.

The principal agents responsible for the ordinary rusting of iron are (*a*) moisture, without which rusting is impossible, (*b*) small proportions of impurities in the iron, which set up electrolytic action, (*c*) oxygen and carbon dioxide from the air, and (*d*) common salt from the ground in which the iron has been buried, from sea air or from dust in the atmosphere.

For cleaning iron from corrosion, when the condition of the object will allow, a simple and satisfactory method is first to remove as much of the rust as possible by brushing with a fine steel-wire brush or by flaking

with a small chisel or hammer as described
when dealing with bronze, and then to place
the object, surrounded by granulated zinc,
in a solution of caustic soda, which is kept
gently simmering, as already described for
bronze. After treatment the object is rinsed
with water and again well brushed with a
steel-wire brush and finally thoroughly
washed, quickly dried and coated with a
preservative varnish as recommended for
bronze. Many iron objects, however, are
too thin or too much corroded to bear
mechanical treatment or reduction, in some
instance being only a mass of oxide, and,
in such cases, all that can be done is to
remove any salt present, well dry the object
and coat it with a preservative varnish.

To remove salt, the object is first soaked
in repeated changes of water until the washings show no salt on testing; it is then soaked
or, better, boiled in a strong solution of
caustic soda or of carbonate of soda, which
is followed by prolonged boiling in water
until all the alkali is washed out. The
object is then thoroughly and quickly dried
by heating and when cold coated with a
preservative varnish. Linseed oil, which
is often used for this purpose, causes great
disfigurement, and is not as efficient as the

varnishes recommended, which also have the advantage of being colourless. All oils, fats and greases, except those of mineral origin, should be avoided on principle, as they are apt to develop acidity on keeping. Vaseline and paraffin wax might be used, but are not needed, as a colourless varnish of the kind mentioned meets all requirements and is an equally efficient protection.

Lead Lead oxidizes quickly in moist air, but the result is only a superficial tarnish. Sometimes, however, ancient lead objects when found are coated with a thick white layer, often of a warty appearance, which consists largely of basic carbonate, with often a small proportion of chloride. Occasionally, too, lead is badly corroded, and even eaten into holes, by having been buried in damp ground containing nitrates.

The best way to clean lead objects is to commence by boiling in repeated changes of water in order to remove any chloride or nitrate present, followed, if there is basic carbonate, by soaking for some hours in a solution (10 per cent.) of acetic acid, after which the object is thoroughly and repeatedly washed in water, dried and coated with a preservative varnish, such as a dilute solution of celluloid or of cellulose acetate.

Papyrus and Paper

Papyrus This is made from the fine layers of fibrous material obtained from the stem of the Egyptian papyrus plant. It was first employed as a writing material by the ancient Egyptians and afterwards by the Greeks and Romans.

Papyrus documents are often very dry and brittle and sometimes impregnated with salt.

No attempt should be made to unfold or to straighten out papyrus while dry, as it would almost certainly break, but it should always first be damped with just sufficient water to render it pliable, which may be done by wrapping it in damp cloth or in damp white blotting-paper and allowing it to remain until the moisture has thoroughly penetrated.

To remove salt, which should always be done when present, there is only one way, namely, to soak the papyrus in repeated changes of pure water until the washings when tested are free from salt. With care, and unless the papyrus is in a very broken condition, water will not injure it, if the soaking is not too prolonged; the water, however, will be coloured brown and the papyrus will become lighter in shade. To allow the water to penetrate freely the papyrus should first be moistened with alcohol. When wet, care must be taken that the ink is not rubbed during handling, as ink comes off very readily from damp papyrus. After removal from the water it is better to soak the papyrus for a few minutes in two changes of pure alcohol; it is then placed between a number of thicknesses of clean white blotting-paper and pressed until dry. Unless alcohol is used after the water, the ink will tend to come off on to the blotting-paper. The alcohol also hastens drying.

Whenever possible papyrus should be mounted between glass, but if for any special reason it should be necessary to fasten it to paper or card, all adhesives except gum or starch paste must be avoided, otherwise should it be desired to remove it at any time, this might be impossible without damage.

Photographic developing dishes make excellent receptacles for use when soaking papyrus in water or other solution.

Paper   Modern paper of the best quality is made from linen and cotton rags, and other qualities from esparto, wood, straw, and other fibrous materials, but old documents are always of linen or cotton.

Paper is not likely to contain salt, but old paper is generally discoloured and frequently dirty, stained and disfigured, and sometimes very brittle.

Discoloration due to age is largely a process of oxidation brought about by natural means, and it takes place in proportion to the extent to which the paper has been exposed to the air and light, and hence the outsides and edges of old documents, which are the most exposed, become the most discoloured, the discoloration progressively diminishing towards the less exposed parts. Other causes for the discoloration of old documents are exposure to dust and dirt, occasional staining by liquids, grease, ink, the excreta of rats, mice and insects and disfigurement by fungus growths, the outsides and edges generally suffering the most. Sometimes isolated brown spots caused by iron or other impurities also occur.

No attempt should be made to bleach the natural discoloration due to age, as this is not unpleasing, and is an evidence of genuineness in a document and any treatment would only tend to make the paper more tender.

Oil and grease may be removed by soaking the paper in petroleum spirit, which is without any injurious effect upon either the paper or the writing and which quickly dries. If soaking is impossible the grease may be largely removed by means of the same reagent applied to the back of the paper on a tuft of cotton-wool. This will always spread the stain to some extent, but generally in such an attenuated form that it will be scarcely visible.

Writing ink as first used was composed of finely divided carbon suspended in water by means of gum, but later (possibly about the fourth century A.D. and certainly by the seventh century) an ink made by mixing an iron compound with an infusion of galls was introduced and gradually superseded the older carbon ink for general use, although for special purposes, and in the East, carbon ink is still employed to some extent. Carbon ink is generally very permanent, but when once removed from the paper it cannot be restored. Iron ink, on the other hand, is not very permanent and gradually becomes brown and faint or fades entirely, but may be restored temporarily by brushing over with a solution of yellow ammonium sulphide or by exposure to the vapours of the same compound, or more permanently by brushing over with a solution of tannic acid in water or of potassium ferrocyanide rendered slightly acid with hydrochloric acid. The latter gives a blue colour, which may be turned brown by treatment with dilute ammonia solution. Stains made by carbon ink are not likely to occur, but if present, may be removed by means of warm water and gentle rubbing. Ink stains, if made anciently by an iron ink, may be removed by applying to the stained area as small a quantity as possible of a dilute solution of oxalic acid or tartaric acid, allowing it to remain a few seconds, soaking up the excess with clean white blotting-paper, repeating the application of acid if necessary, and finally well washing by applying drops of water several times and each time soaking up the water with blotting-paper. Stains made with a modern blue-black ink, which is an iron ink containing a blue colouring matter, generally an aniline dye, may be removed by applying alternately oxalic acid (or tartaric acid) and a dilute solution of bleaching powder (or of sodium hypochlorite), the excess solution being soaked up with blotting-paper and the places finally well washed with water as already described.

Fungus growths on old paper are frequently dead, but if not they may be killed, and so prevented from spreading, by brushing the places attacked with a solution of thymol in alcohol or in petroleum spirit or by immersing the paper in these solutions.

Photographic developing dishes make excellent receptacles for use when immersing documents in a solution of any sort. Should it be necessary for any special reason to soak a document in water, it should be laid on a sheet of glass slightly smaller than the dish, so that in removing it from the water it may be lifted out on the glass without the paper being touched, as wet paper is very tender and tears easily. In the absence of a sheet of glass, the water should be poured off carefully and the document left in the dish to dry, when it may be removed with safety.

Parchment and Vellum Parchment and vellum are essentially the same material, and are both made from the skins of animals, the former from the skins of sheep and goats, and the latter, which is of finer quality, from the more delicate skins of calves and kids.

Both parchment and vellum swell when wetted, and therefore cannot be cleaned with water, but may be cleaned with petroleum spirit applied on a tuft of cotton-wool.

Pictures *Paint.*—Paint is of so many different kinds and varies so much, not only in respect to the material on which it is executed but also in the nature of the pigments employed, that no general methods, either of cleaning or preserving it, are possible. The subject is also so large and to a great extent beyond the scope of the present book that a few aspects of it only will be considered.

Cleaning.—The method of cleaning paint depends upon many factors, including not only the nature of the ground upon which it occurs, but also the nature of the priming, pigments, medium and varnish employed. Paint which has been varnished, or which has been executed in wax, or coated with wax, may be cleaned from dust and dirt by first brushing carefully with a camel-hair or other soft brush, and then sponging with a small damp sponge or damp tuft of cotton-wool or brushing with a soft damp brush.

Unvarnished paint should not be cleaned with water, as this would also generally remove the pigment, but may be cleaned by means of petroleum spirit or alcohol, which are best applied on a tuft of cotton-wool or with a camel-hair or other similar soft brush. Petroleum spirit, too, is generally safe to use on varnish, but not on wax, while with alcohol the reverse is the case, and this may be used on wax, but not on varnish.

Preservation.—As both the material on which the painting is executed and the pigments employed may require preservative treatment, these will be separately considered.

Materials of Ground.—The materials on which painting is done comprise canvas, gesso, paper, papyrus, plaster, stone and wood. Most of these materials will be described in other connections, as also the damage to which they are subject and the methods of preventing damage or the remedy when it is too late for prevention. A little repetition, however, may not be out of place.

Canvas, paper and papyrus, if kept in a damp place, are all liable to be attacked by fungus growths. The first remedy, therefore, is to remove the object to dry surroundings, and then, if possible, to treat it with something that will kill the fungi without injuring the material. Many otherwise excellent fungicides are inadmissible on account of their being water solutions, or because they are liable to slow decomposition with the production of bodies that would destroy the material on which it was used, canvas paper and papyrus being very susceptible to the action of even small quantities of acid substances and of chlorine. Thymol, which has been proposed by Dr. Alexander Scott,[1]

[1] *The Cleaning and Restoration of Museum Exhibits,* Dept. of Sci. and Ind. Research, London, 1921.

for destroying fungus growths on prints, is also both safe and satisfactory for paper other than 'prints, and also for canvas and papyrus. The object is enclosed in an airtight case and exposed to the vapour of thymol, which is a solid body easily volatilized on gently heating, which may be done by means of an electric lamp.

Gesso and plaster, both being injured by moisture, must be kept dry, but gesso on wood should not be dried too much, otherwise the wood shrinks and the gesso breaks off. Gesso on wood may be consolidated by impregnating it with melted paraffin wax. This, however, always darkens wood and therefore alters the colour values of any pigments present.

Wood is liable to be attacked by boring beetles, the best remedy for which, in the case of small museum objects which are painted, is fumigation with carbon disulphide, which when pure has no deleterious effect on the pigments.

Pigments.—Many pigments are acted upon injuriously by light, and therefore need to be protected, not only from direct sunlight, but also from too great an exposure to diffused daylight. There are, however, exceptions to this, and in some cases the exclusion of light is harmful and not beneficial. Thus certain paints are liable to darken in the absence of light, and it is a common experience in Egypt to see paint on woodwork quite white where exposed to light and discoloured and yellowish where protected from light, as for example on walls beneath pictures and on the inner sides of doors standing permanently open against walls.

Many pigments too are acted upon injuriously by moisture and particularly when the moisture carries in solution sulphur acids, such as are generated by the burning of coal and coal gas. Protection both from moisture and sulphur compounds, however, is not a difficult matter, and consists in proper attention to heating and ventilation, together with the exclusion of gas lighting and gas fires.

In cases in which a pigment has faded or changed colour, nothing as a rule can be done to restore it. To this, however, there is one exception, namely, when the pigment is white lead (flake white) which has become discoloured by sulphur compounds. The black sulphide of lead formed may be converted (oxidized) into white sulphate by means of hydrogen peroxide, but this reagent cannot safely be used if pigments other than white lead are present, as some of the other colours might be injured. The simplest way of applying hydrogen peroxide is in the form of a solution in either water or ether, and preferably the latter, which is painted on the blackened pigment with a camel-hair brush. This same method may be applied to blackened white lead on illuminated manuscripts.

Unvarnished paint on gesso, plaster, stone and wood may be protected and caused to adhere again by spraying with a dilute solution of celluloid or of cellulose acetate.

In connection with paint, the black paint-like coating on many ancient Egyptian wooden funerary objects, already referred to, may again be mentioned. This is not a paint, but a kind of varnish, consisting of a natural black resin of a lacquer-like character, such as is found and used in India, China and Japan at the present day. It was applied directly to the wood, and sometimes is not now very adherent. Being a resin it is soluble in such reagents as alcohol and acetone, and if sprayed with either of these solvents, should it show signs of flaking off, it softens at the edges and adheres again. The spraying makes the surface very glossy, but in many instances this was the original appearance.

Pottery By pottery is meant vessels and ware made from clay and then hardened by being baked ; it may be either glazed or unglazed ; Egyptian faience and porcelain are not included.

Pottery is very resistant to the ordinary processes of decay, and its weakness lies in its fragility and often in its porosity, the latter being characteristic of unglazed pottery.

The fragility of pottery allows it to be easily broken and the porosity permits it to become impregnated with various substances, fatty matter, for instance, in the case of jars containing fat, or salts from salty ground, which latter may ultimately cause disintegration if the salts should have an opportunity of crystallizing.

Pottery is sometimes disfigured by incrustations of carbonate or sulphate of lime, or both, derived from wet ground containing these substances.

As a rule the first step towards cleaning pottery is to wash it well with water and a soft brush. If salt is present the object must be soaked in repeated changes of pure water until all the salt is dissolved out. This will take some days and possibly several weeks.

Fatty matter may be removed by soaking the object in petroleum spirit, but it must be dry before treatment.

No attempt should be made to remove either carbonate or sulphate of lime by scraping, as this would not only be useless, but might also scratch or disfigure the object. Carbonate of lime may be removed by brushing it repeatedly with a dilute solution of hydrochloric acid (2 to 5 per cent.). Sulphate of lime generally falls off during soaking in water to dissolve out salt or softens sufficiently to be readily detached, but may be removed by treatment with hydrochloric acid in the same way as for carbonate. After acid, the object must be washed in repeated changes of water until no trace of acid remains. Baking will cause sulphate of lime to crumble to powder and fall off, but frequently the object is too large for baking to be conveniently applied.

The exceptions to the above-mentioned methods of treatment are objects that have been painted after having been fired and also fragments of pottery bearing written inscriptions. Although these may generally be soaked in water without damage, if the soaking is not too prolonged, this must not be taken for granted, and they should be well watched for some time after being placed in the water. Great care is necessary in handling painted pottery, or pottery bearing ink inscriptions, while wet, as both paint and ink then easily rub off.

It is well known that an ink inscription on pottery (also on stone or wood) is more visible when wet, and therefore inscriptions are often wetted in order that they may be deciphered. This is most unwise, and is very liable to destroy the inscription. A perfectly safe way of bringing up ink inscriptions is to spray them with petroleum spirit or alcohol. The effect, as with water, is only temporary, but the treatment may be repeated as often as necessary without danger.

Acid should never be used on painted pottery until it has been proved by an experiment on one small portion that it will not injure the colour.

Pottery may be repaired with celluloid cement if the objects are small, but in the case of large objects, glue or plaster of Paris suitably tinted should be used. Missing portions may be replaced by tinted plaster, which is afterwards treated with celluloid, cellulose acetate, paraffin wax or stearine as already described.[1]

Stone The stone used in antiquity was of many different kinds, the principal varieties being alabaster (calcite), limestone, marble, sand-

[1] Pp. 19–22.

stone and igneous rocks, such as basalt, diorite, dolerite and granite. In many instances stone objects have been exposed to atmospheric influences during thousands of years and a certain amount of disintegration has been produced, chiefly by variations of temperature, the mechanical action of wind-borne particles of sand and the solvent action of water, generally rain containing carbon dioxide in solution. The damage cannot be remedied, but as soon as the stone is removed from the sphere of action of the agents mentioned disintegration ceases. In addition, however, to the causes of damage enumerated, there is one other factor, which is the most potent of all, and which is largely responsible for the disintegration and destruction of limestone and sandstone in dry countries such as Egpyt, chiefly because these two stones are soft and porous. This destructive agent is salt, which consists largely of chloride of sodium (common salt), but sometimes is a mixture of common salt and sulphate of soda, with occasionally small proportions of other salts, such as carbonate of soda, nitrate of soda and nitrate of potash. The action of salt on stone is not analagous to its action on metals, and as a rule is not chemical, but entirely physical, and is caused by the salt crystallizing underneath the surface layers of the stone, which are forced off by the irresistible expansion consequent on the crystallization. For such action to take place four conditions are necessary, namely, firstly, the presence of water-soluble salts, secondly, the presence of water to dissolve the salts, thirdly, porous stone, and fourthly, opportunity for the salts to be brought to the surface of the stone by capillary attraction and there to crystallize out, owing to the evaporation of the water holding them in solution.

With the exception of limestone, very few stones naturally contain more than a trace of soluble salts, but limestone may contain several per cent., and the author has found as much as 4·6 per cent. of water-soluble salts in a specimen of limestone taken direct from the quarry. As a rule, however, when stone contains much salt, this has been derived from salty ground in which the stone has lain.

Excepting limestone and sandstone, few stones are very porous, and therefore generally it is only these two kinds of stone that contain salt. When a stone is quite dry, salt is harmless, but it is almost impossible to keep a salty stone dry, since salt attracts and absorbs water even from a damp atmosphere.

Since the salts causing mischief are soluble in water the obvious way of removing them is to soak the stone in water until it is free from salt. In many cases, however, this cannot be done, because the object is too large and in other cases it is only possible to do it without damage if certain precautions have been taken, on account of the stone having a plaster surface or bearing a painted inscription, or both. In those cases in which soaking is possible and permissible, the object should be entirely immersed in water contained in a stone or cement basin or in a wooden box lined with lead or zinc, but not in iron or tinned iron. The object should be raised above the bottom of the vessel, preferably on brick or stone supports, but not on metal, as such metals as iron or copper would discolour the stone. The water must be changed frequently until on testing it is found to be free from more than a trace of salt. This will take many weeks and often months. The stone when removed from the water is allowed to dry slowly in a warm place. In this connection it should not be forgotten that water has a slight solvent action on limestone, and with prolonged soaking the sharp outlines of carvings and inscriptions may suffer. The growth of algæ, which tend to develop, especially in warm weather, may be prevented by frequent changing of the water, by covering the vessel so as to exclude the light, and by dissolving in the water a very small proportion of copper sulphate.

Sometimes patches of crystals of sulphate of lime occur on stone objects that have been buried in damp ground. Any such crystals will either fall off during soaking in water or will so soften that they may readily be detached. Acids should not be used, as they act vigorously upon limestone and dissolve it and, even in the case of sandstone, the material cementing together the grains of sand will probably contain carbonate of lime and this would be attacked by acid.

Stone objects, which bear painted inscriptions, must on no account be wetted until the painted surface has been protected from the action of water, or the paint will probably be destroyed. The necessary protection may be given by spraying or otherwise treating the surface of the stone with some material that is insoluble in, and unacted upon by, water. Such substances are celluloid, cellulose acetate, dammar resin, mastic resin and shellac, a description of which, with the manner of making and using, has already been given.[1] Preservatives of unknown composition should never be employed, and all substances such as silicate of soda (water glass), silicate of potash, silico-fluorides (fluosilicates, fluates) and baryta should be avoided, not only because they can only be used in aqueous solution, but also because they generally form a thin skin on the surface of the stone which eventually scales off, while as a secondary effect they often cause an efflorescence of salt which increases any disintegration taking place. Linseed oil, which is sometimes advocated, should not be used, as it darkens the colour of the stone.

Occasionally limestone naturally contains veinlets of common salt, or is so largely impregnated with salt that it is barely holding together. In such cases washing with water would be fatal and the only remedy is to treat the stone with a preservative without attempting to remove the salt. When the disintegration is less pronounced the object may be wrapped in gauze or bound round with fine string before being soaked.

Sometimes objects bearing painted inscrip-

[1] Pp. 30–32.

tions have a layer of plaster under the paint or have had irregularities in the stone smoothed over with plaster. Such objects cannot be wetted without the plaster coming off, and if salty they must be treated with one of the preservative solutions mentioned without any attempt being made to remove the salt.

Black spots, which occasionally disfigure limestone, but more often sandstone, are generally due to oxide of manganese or mixed oxides of iron and manganese, natural to the stone, and cannot be remedied.

Sometimes stone objects are wantonly disfigured, and in such cases the method of treatment naturally depends upon the nature of the material used. In one instance in Egypt the walls of a number of chambers in the Temple of Rameses II at Abydos were smeared with a black material which proved to be a carbon writing ink. The greater part of this was removed by sponging with water, but in places a 5 per cent. solution of carbonate of soda was used. The report states that on the whole the treatment was successful, but that there was a slight *dégradation* of the colour of the paint.[1]

[1] *Annales du Service des Antiquités de l'Egypte.* Tome xii. Le Caire, 1912.

The carbonate of soda, however, was unnecessary, and might have caused damage.

In this connection a brief record of what has actually been done in the way of preservative treatment of painted surfaces on stone and plaster may be useful, and the following have been traced :

1. The paintings on the walls of tomb No. 22 (Wah) at Thebes which were rapidly disappearing owing to the powdery state of the colours were sprayed three times, first with a weak and then with a strong solution of albumen. It is stated that this has effectually fixed the colours, that no stain or darkening has been caused, and that, owing to the colours being painted directly on the stone, there is no danger that the albumen will be attacked by white ants.[1]

2. The colours on the plaster of the Tel-el-Amarna pavement were fixed by means of tapioca water, applied just thick enough to soak entirely in without leaving any glair on the surface.[2]

3. The limestone blocks forming the tomb

[1] *Annales du Service des Antiquités de l'Egypte.* Tome xiv. Le Caire, 1914.

[2] *Tel-el-Amarna.* W. H. Flinders Petrie, London, 1894.

of Perneb, which was removed from Egypt and re-erected in the Metropolitan Museum of Art, New York, were being damaged by an efflorescence of salt.   Immersion in water was impossible owing to the presence of plaster, which had been freely used to fill out and conceal imperfections in the stone, and the painted surfaces of the blocks were therefore treated " in such a way as to bottle up the salts. . . ." [1]   The preparation used is a proprietary one, but it is believed that it contains Chinese wood oil, resin and fatty acids.

In the author's opinion a solution of celluloid is preferable to any of the three materials mentioned and also more efficacious.   Fatty acids should certainly be avoided, as they cannot fail to have some, though possibly only slight, solvent action on limestone.

As a rule, stone objects are best repaired with plaster of Paris suitably tinted, unless the object is small, when celluloid cement should be used.

Textile Fabrics   Textile fabrics vary very much in their state of preservation, being at times in excellent condition and at other times badly decayed and falling to powder.

[1] *The Tomb of Perneb*, New York, 1916.

The reason for the disintegration of textile fabrics is not fully understood, but the factors which appear to be of importance in this connection are air, heat and humidity, and it seems probable that the changes are partly chemical and partly biological, the chemical action being in the nature of oxidation and the biological effects being brought about by bacteria and fungi (moulds).

When textile fabrics are in a good state of preservation, but contain salt, as may happen in wrappings or garments on bodies that have been treated either with natron or salt, the salt may be removed by soaking in repeated changes of pure water. Soaking in water, however, would be fatal to fabrics in a tender condition.

Merely ironing a textile fabric, with or without slight damping, will often considerably improve and strengthen it.

The best way to strengthen fabrics which are in a tender condition, is to spray them with a solution of celluloid or of cellulose acetate. On no account should paraffin wax be used, as it masks all pattern and colour and is a great disfigurement.

To prevent the attacks of insects and moulds, textile fabrics should be kept in well-fitting cases in a dry atmosphere and should be sprayed with a solution of mercuric chloride in alcohol, which must be used with care, as it is very poisonous, or with a solution of naphthalene in carbon tetrachloride. If actually attacked, the best remedy is fumigation with carbon disulphide, which may be carried out by exposing this reagent in open dishes in the cases and allowing it to evaporate. Solid naphthalene in the case confers a limited degree of protection against certain kinds of insects.

Wood   Wood is subject to many ills, including the attacks of insects and fungi, the action of water-soluble salts and staining by oil. These will now be considered.

Insects.—The principal insects that destroy dead wood (excluding marine woodboring molluscs and crustaceans) are white ants (termites) and several kinds of boring beetle.

The white ant is sometimes found infecting ancient tombs, as in certain parts of Thebes and at Tel-el-Amarna, and in such cases there is no remedy, since the mischief will already have been done before the tomb or other excavation is opened, and wooden objects, unless they are made of a few certain kinds of wood which seem to be immune, will be entirely destroyed when found. Museums, too, are occasionally invaded by white ants. When there is any danger of this the enemy may be kept out by the following mentioned precautions, namely, (*a*) clear spaces covered with sand, gravel, stone, brick or asphalt surrounding the building, (*b*) all woodwork to be insulated from the ground by at least a foot of stone, burned brick or concrete; (*c*) floors to be of stone, cement or tiles and not of wood; (*d*) show-cases and wooden objects resting on the floor to be protected by metal sheeting underneath. Other remedies, such as tar, creosote and paint also protect wood against white ants, but cannot be applied to antique objects.

Boring beetles may be kept out of wooden objects by well-fitting show-cases. If an object is already infected, the best remedy for ordinary application to small objects is fumigation with carbon disulphide. This may be done in the show-case itself by leaving some of the liquid exposed for a week or two so that it will evaporate and saturate the air and also the contents of the case. Carbon disulphide being volatile and very inflammable, special precautions must be taken against fire. Other methods that may be employed are spraying with a solution of mercuric chloride in alcohol, with benzol or with naphthalene dissolved in carbon tetrachloride.

Fungi.—The well-known decay of wood called " Dry Rot " is caused by several kinds of fungi. The term, however, is a misnomer, and the decay is not due to the wood being dry, since moisture must be present before the fungi will grow, but to the dry powdery appearance of the wood when badly attacked. The conditions that are most favourable to the production of dry rot are a warm, moist and stagnant atmosphere. The preventives are good ventilation and spraying with a fungicide, such as a solution of mercuric chloride in alcohol. Fungicides dissolved in water are not recommended, as all wetting of wood should be avoided whenever possible.

Salts.—It is not very usual to find salts in wooden objects, but they occur occasionally, and are always derived from the ground in which the objects have been buried. When salts are present it is chiefly in the form of common salt, though Scott mentions [1] a case in which wooden objects were impregnated with ammonium compounds derived

[1] *The Cleaning and Restoration of Museum Exhibits*, Dept. of Sci. and Ind. Research, London, 1923.

from guano. Although when dealing with wooden objects the use of water should be avoided if possible, there are instances, such as the presence of salt, where the only remedy is to soak the object in water or in a water solution : for example, to remove the ammonium salts mentioned Scott used dilute acetic acid followed by washing in water. After having been wetted the objects must be dried carefully and above all, slowly. This is essential. Soaking in alcohol after the water helps drying. If objects have been found in water or in a damp situation it is difficult to dry them in the ordinary way without warping, and in such cases the best method is to place them on a grating in a vessel containing paraffin oil (kerosene) and allow them to remain until all the water has been replaced by oil. They are then immersed in petroleum spirit until this in turn displaces the paraffin oil. The objects should then be well drained and dried and impregnated with hot melted paraffin wax. Paraffin wax, the use of which is due to Flinders Petrie, is one of the most valuable remedies for the treatment of wooden objects in a bad state of preservation. If possible, the object should be well warmed before applying the wax ; if the object is warm and the wax very hot the wax all soaks in without leaving any excess on the surface to cause disfigurement. However, should any surplus be left, this may be removed by heat or by means of a soft cloth or a soft brush soaked in petroleum spirit. Wax has one great drawback, namely, that it darkens wood, and if the wood is painted, but not varnished, this darkening shows through and alters the colour values of the pigments, white especially being much darkened. On a painted but varnished surface wax has no darkening effect.

Oil.—Oil or grease may be removed by soaking the object in benzol or in petroleum spirit, or, if this is not possible, the stains should be treated with either of these solvents applied with a rag.

CHAPTER IV

SIMPLE PHYSICAL AND CHEMICAL TESTS

Physical Tests

Detailed physical examination or chemical testing are matters for the specialist, but the knowledge of how to carry out a few simple tests will be advantageous alike to the archæologist, the curator and the collector. A few tests therefore will be described. The physical tests should be done before the chemical ones, as generally the amount of material available is limited. The materials mentioned are those likely to occur in connection with antique objects.

The physical tests are as follows :

1. Examination with a lens.
2. Hardness.
3. Fracture.
4. Specific Gravity.

These will now be considered in detail.

Examination with a Lens From the examination of a material with a lens much may be learned, and details of colour, structure and composition not visible

to the naked eye may be seen. Specimens
of known and likely materials should be
examined alongside the doubtful material.
A good hand lens or a watchmaker's eye-
glass is recommended.

Hardness   Hardness is a most useful test for the
examination of mineral substances. The
hardness may be determined in several
different ways: firstly, by scratching the
material with the thumb-nail; secondly, by
scratching it with the point of a penknife;
thirdly, by rubbing the material on a small,
fine, clean, hard file and noting the extent to
which it is affected, and fourthly, by scratching the material with various minerals of
known hardness.

The hardness of a mineral is expressed
by a number. The following tabular state-
ment shows the hardness of the principal
materials likely to occur. The thumb-nail
will scratch minerals of a hardness not
exceeding 2·5, and a penknife will scratch
minerals up to a hardness of about 5·5, thus
gypsum may be easily scratched with the
nail, whereas alabaster (calcite) requires a
knife to scratch it and quartz cannot be
scratched even with a knife, which means
that it is harder than steel. The minerals
with a hardness of 6 will just scratch window

glass, while those with a hardness of 7 or
upwards scratch glass easily. When a
mineral neither scratches nor is scratched
by a particular substance the hardness of
the two is the same. After making a scratch
the powder should be wiped off and the
surface examined with a lens in order to
make sure that the powder does not come
from the scratching agent, which may happen when the two substances are of nearly
the same hardness.

TABLE OF HARDNESS

Number	Material
1	Steatite.
2	Gypsum.
2·5	Amber, galena.
3	Alabaster (calcite).
3·5	Malachite.
4	Serpentine.
5·5	Glass, lapis lazuli, obsidian.
6	Feldspar, hæmatite, turquoise.
7	Agate, amethyst, carnelian, chalcedony, flint, jasper, quartz, rock crystal.
7·5	Aquamarine, beryl, emerald.
8	Topaz.
9	Sapphire.
10	Diamond.

Fracture The nature of the fracture produced when
minerals and other materials are broken is
very characteristic. Examples of different
kinds of fracture are as follows :

1. *Conchoidal.*—When the broken surface

is curved, either convex or concave. Examples : Amber, flint, glass, obsidian, quartz.

2. *Even.*—When the surface is flat or nearly so. Example : Chert.

3. *Earthy.*—Example : Chalk.

Specific Gravity The specific gravity of a substance is the ratio of its weight to that of an equal volume of water. The small variations due to differences of temperature may be neglected in determinations such as those under consideration.

The ordinary laboratory methods of determining the specific gravity of a solid body by weighing first in air and then in water, or by ascertaining the loss of weight in water from the weight of water displaced, cannot be employed in the absence of the necessary apparatus, and as this is not usually possessed by archæologists or curators the methods become impracticable. Two other methods, however, are very simple, and require only such apparatus as may readily be obtained. The results, although only approximate, are sufficiently accurate for the purpose required. The methods are as follows :

1. If the object is of a regular shape that may be easily measured, such as an oblong or square, measure three dimensions (height,

width and depth) and calculate the cubic
contents, then weigh it and calculate the
weight per cubic centimetre or per cubic
inch. Since 1 cubic centimetre of water
weighs 1 gram (15·4 grains) and 1 cubic
inch of water weighs 16·4 grams (252·6
grains), the gravity may readily be calculated.
This does not allow for any air present, and
therefore with porous objects represents the
apparent and not the real specific gravity.

2. By measuring the displaced water.
Take a small glass cylinder graduated in
cubic centimetres, partly fill it with water
and note the volume, then carefully put the
object into the water and again note the
level of the water. The difference between
the two readings is the volume of water in
cubic centimetres displaced by the object.
But since 1 cubic centimetre of water
weighs 1 gram, the volume in cubic centimetres also represents the weight in grams.
The specific gravity of the object is its weight
in grams divided by the weight of water
displaced, also in grams. If the object is a
large one, the experiment may be done in a
beaker, the two water levels being marked
by strips of gummed paper and the water
displaced poured into a graduated cylinder
for measurement.

The specific gravities of a few materials are given in the following table :

Specific Gravity	Material
1·1	Amber.
2·3	Gypsum.
2·4 to 2·5	Lapis lazuli.
2·5 to 2·6	Obsidian, serpentine.
2·5 to 3	Glass.
2·6	Agate, amethyst, carnelian, chalcedony, jasper, quartz, rock crystal.
2·6 to 2·8	Feldspar, turquoise.
2·7	Alabaster (calcite), beryl, emerald.
2·7 to 2·8	Steatite.
2·9	Aragonite.
3·5	Topaz.
3·5 to 4	Malachite.
5·0	Hæmatite.
7·5	Galena.

CHEMICAL TESTS

The apparatus required for the chemical tests consists of a few small test-tubes, a few watch glasses, some thin iron wire and blue and red litmus paper. The chemical reagents required, together with the strengths of the solutions to be used, will be found described later.

The tests are as follows :

1. Solubility.

2. Behaviour on heating.

3. Reaction with acid.

4. Testing of solutions formed when the material is soluble in water or acid.

5. Flame coloration.

These will now be described. Before undertaking any chemical tests it should be seen that all reagents are pure and all apparatus thoroughly clean.

Solubility For solubility a small quantity of the material is powdered finely and tested to see whether it is soluble, first, in water (distilled if possible), secondly, in alcohol, and thirdly, in petroleum spirit. This may be done on a watch glass or in a small test-tube.

Soluble in Water.—Carbonate of soda, nitrate of soda, sulphate of soda, nitrate of potash (saltpetre), salt (common salt, rock salt). Glue and gum are first softened by water and then dissolved. Clay disintegrates in water and feels soapy.

Soluble in Alcohol.—Resin, resin varnish, wood pitch.

Soluble in Petroleum Spirit.—Bitumen, fat, grease, mineral pitch, oils.

Behaviour on Heating To apply the heating test place a small piece of the material on the point of a penknife and heat in the flame of a gas-jet, spirit-lamp or candle. Note (*a*) whether the material melts, (*b*) whether the material burns, and if so whether it burns freely, (*c*) the smell produced, and (*d*) the nature of the residue, if any. If the material melts before it burns it is possibly fat, resin or wax (beeswax). Smear it while melted on a piece of white paper. A greasy stain indicates either fat or wax. If the material burns it is most probably organic, although it should not be forgotten that some inorganic substances, sulphur for example, also burn. Other inorganic materials, such as ammonium chloride, disappear when heated by volatilization and not by burning. The smell of the burning material is often very characteristic, and bitumen, fats, mineral pitch, oils, resin, sulphur and nitrogenous matters (hair, horn, mummy flesh) may all be identified by the smell.

Reaction with Acid To test the reaction with acid, take a few small fragments or scrapings if the object is one that may be cut or scraped, powder them finely, and place a little of the powder in a small test-tube and pour on it a little dilute hydrochloric acid and watch the result. If the object may not be cut or scraped, place on it in an inconspicuous place (by means of a small pipette or a fine glass rod) a small drop of dilute hydrochloric acid and watch the result with a lens.

The following named are soluble with effervescence : Alabaster (calcite), carbonate of lime, chalk, limestone, malachite (forming a green solution), marble, whiting.

The following named is soluble without effervescence : Sulphate of lime (gypsum).

Testing of Solutions

Water Solution.—The solution formed by dissolving any material in water should be tested as follows :

1. For alkalinity and acidity, which may be done by means of litmus paper. If the solution is alkaline, red litmus turns blue, whereas if the solution is acid, blue litmus becomes red.

Alkalinity in connection with antique objects generally signifies natron (which contains carbonate of soda). Acidity is unusual, and not likely to occur in a water solution.

2. For the presence of chloride, which will generally indicate common salt or natron (which contains salt).

Chloride is tested for by means of nitrate of silver. To a little of the solution contained in a test tube or in a watch glass add a few drops of a solution of nitrate of silver. A milkiness indicates a trace of chloride and a curdy precipitate means a larger amount. This should be confirmed by adding a few drops of dilute nitric acid, which should not produce any change, that is to say, the milkiness or precipitate should not disappear. Ordinary pure water contains a trace of chloride, and well water often contains a considerable amount.

3. For the presence of sulphate, which will generally indicate sulphate of soda, but may mean sulphate of magnesia.

Sulphate is tested for by means of chloride of barium. To a little of the water solution contained in a small test-tube or in a watch glass add a few drops of a solution of chloride of barium. A slight cloudiness appearing after a time indicates a trace of sulphate, a heavy white precipitate indicating a larger amount. This should be confirmed by adding a few drops of dilute hydrochloric acid, which should not dissolve the precipitate. Care should be taken not to make the solution too acid, otherwise the hydrochloric acid will produce a precipitate, which, however, disappears on diluting with water.

Acid Solution.—This should be tested for sulphate in the same manner as described for the water solution. A precipitate with chloride of barium indicates sulphate, which, in the absence of sulphate in the water solution, will generally mean sulphate of lime (gypsum). Chloride cannot be tested for in the acid solution, as the acid itself would give the reaction.

Flame Coloration For the flame coloration test scrape off a little of the material, place it on a watch glass and add a few drops of strong hydrochloric acid. Dip the end of a thin piece of clean iron wire in the solution and hold it in the outer zone of the flame, about one-third of the way up, and note the colour produced. This may be as follows :

Yellow.—This is the most common, and indicates sodium compounds, but as these are so widely distributed, occurring even in the dust in the air, a yellow coloration, unless very vivid, may be disregarded. Without other tests it is impossible to say what particular sodium compound is present.

Red.—This indicates calcium compounds, such as alabaster, gypsum, limestone, and whiting.

Blue and Green.—These indicate copper compounds.

Beeswax.—Almost insoluble in alcohol, slightly soluble in petroleum spirit, soluble in chloroform and in carbon disulphide, melts when heated, burns with a smoky flame and gives a characteristic smell.

Summary of Results of Chemical Tests

Bitumen (Mineral Pitch). — Insoluble or only slightly soluble in alcohol, soluble in petroleum spirit, giving a brown solution, burns with a smoky flame, giving a characteristic smell.

Carbonate of Lime.—This occurs as alabaster (calcite), chalk, limestone, marble, whiting. It is soluble with vigorous effervescence in hydrochloric acid, and the solution imparts a red colour to the flame.

Carbonate of Soda.—Soluble in water, soluble in hydrochloric acid with strong effervescence, imparts a very vivid yellow colour to the flame, water solution alkaline to litmus.

Glue.—Softened and finally dissolved by water, the solution frothing readily on agitation, insoluble in alcohol, gives a disagreeable nitrogenous smell on burning.

Gum.—Soluble in water, insoluble in alcohol, does not melt but chars on heating, no nitrogenous smell on burning.

Lapis lazuli.—This is a double silicate of aluminium and sodium associated with sulphide of sodium and contains patches of carbonate of lime, and often iron pyrites. It is soluble in strong hydrochloric acid, sulphuretted hydrogen being evolved and the white patches giving effervescence.

Malachite.—This is hydrated carbonate of copper. It is soluble in hydrochloric acid with effervescence, giving a green solution of chloride of copper which imparts a blue coloration to the flame. Copper compounds, other than chloride, colour the flame green. Bright steel, such as the blade of a knife, introduced into the hydrochloric acid solution becomes covered with a thin coating of metallic copper.

Natron.—This is a compound of carbonate and bicarbonate of soda, which occurs naturally in Egypt and was used by the ancient Egyptians in embalming; it always contains an admixture of common salt and sulphate of soda, and therefore will give the reactions for these substances. It imparts a very vivid yellow colour to the flame and is alkaline to litmus.

Resin.—Soluble in strong alcohol, insoluble in water, insoluble or only slightly soluble in petroleum spirit, melts with heat, burns with a smoky flame, giving a characteristic smell like burning varnish.

Salt (Chloride of Sodium).—Soluble in water, the solution giving a white precipitate with nitrate of silver, which is insoluble in nitric acid; neutral to litmus, gives a very vivid yellow flame coloration.

Sulphate of Lime (Gypsum).—Soluble in hydrochloric acid without effervescence, though not very readily unless heated; the solution imparts a red colour to the flame.

Sulphate of Soda.—Soluble in water, the solution giving a white precipitate with chloride of barium, which is insoluble in hydrochloric acid; neutral to litmus, and gives a very vivid yellow colour to the flame.

Reagents and Solutions Required

Only the best quality materials should be employed. Using makeshift or inferior materials (and tools) when good quality ones are readily obtainable is false economy of the worst kind, and cannot fail to affect adversely the quality of the work.

The following list contains the description of all the most necessary reagents and solutions required :

Acetone, redistilled	For dissolving celluloid and cellulose acetate.
Acetic acid, glacial	10 per cent. solution in water for cleaning bronze.
Acid formic, about 90 per cent.	From 5 to 25 per cent. solution in water for cleaning silver.
Acid hydrochloric, pure	(a) 1 to 5 per cent. solution in water for dissolving carbonates.
	(b) 10 per cent. solution in water for testing.
Acid nitric, pure .	10 per cent. solution in water for testing.

Acid oxalic, pure .	5 per cent. solution in water for taking out ink stains.
Acid tartaric, pure .	5 per cent. solution in water for taking out ink stains.
Alcohol, rectified spirit or good quality methylated spirit at least 90 per cent. strength	For cleaning and dissolving.
Ammonia solution, pure, specific gravity, 880	For cleaning. Generally used in 10 per cent. solution.
Ammonium chloride, battery crystals.	For cleaning bronze.
Ammonium sulphide solution (sulph-hydrate)	For developing iron ink.
Ammonium sulphite	For cleaning silver.
Amyl acetate, pure	For dissolving celluloid.
Barium chloride, pure	10 per cent. solution in water for testing.
Benzol, pure . .	For cleaning. The more correct name is benzene, but this is liable to be mistaken for benzine.
Benzine, good quality	Aviation spirit, petroleum spirit, petrol. For cleaning.

Bleaching powder . Must be fresh. For taking out ink stains.

Calcium chloride, pure, granular As a drying agent in museum cases.

Canada balsam, best quality For impregnating enamels.

Carbon disulphide, pure As an insecticide.

Carbon tetrachloride, pure For dissolving naphthalene.

Caustic soda, pure, sticks 10 per cent. solution in water for cleaning bronze and iron.

Celluloid, cuttings . For varnish, impregnation and cement.

Cellulose acetate, soluble in acetone For varnish, impregnation and cement.

Copper sulphate, crystals For cleaning silver.

Copper sulphite (cuprous) For cleaning silver.

Dammar resin . . For varnish.

Kerosene, water-white Paraffin oil.

Mastic resin . . For varnish.

Mercuric chloride, powder Corrosive sublimate. Used in 2 per cent. solution in alcohol as an insecticide.

Naphthalene, flake or marbles As an insecticide.

Paraffin wax, melting-point about 60° C. (140° F.)	For impregnation.
Paraffin oil, water-white	Kerosene.
Petroleum spirit, good quality	Benzine, petrol, aviation spirit. For cleaning.
Potassium cyanide, about 90 per cent.	5 per cent. solution in water for cleaning gold and silver.
Rochelle salt, powder	Sodium potassium tartrate. 15 per cent. solution in water for cleaning bronze.
Shellac, bleached .	For varnish.
Sodium sulphide, crystals	Used in dilute solution in water for darkening bronze.
Sodium sulphite, anhydrous	For cleaning silver.
Thymol	As a fungicide.
Tin chloride (stannous), pure	For cleaning bronze.
Water	(a) Distilled for testing. (b) Ordinary pure for washing.

BIBLIOGRAPHY

HARMER, Sir SYDNEY F. " Experiments on the Fading of Museum Specimens." *The Museums Journal,* Vol. 21. London, 1922.

HIORNS, A. H. *Metal Colouring and Bronzing.* London, 1920.

PETRIE, Sir FLINDERS. *Methods and Aims in Archæology.* London, 1904.

RATHGEN, Dr. F. *The Preservation of Antiquities.* Translated by G. A. and H. A. Auden. Cambridge, 1905.

RHOUSONPOULOS, O. A. " On the Cleaning and Preservation of Antiquities." *The Museums Journal,* Vol. 11. London, 1911–12.

ROSENBERG, G. A. *Antiquités en Fer et en Bronze, leur Transformation . . . et leur Conservation.* Copenhagen, 1917.

RUSSELL, W. J., and ABNEY, W. DE W. " Action of Light on Water-Colours." *Blue Book.* London, 1888.

SCOTT, Dr. ALEXANDER. *The Cleaning and Restoration of Museum Exhibits.* First Report, London, 1921 ; Second Report, London, 1923.

INDEX

134

ACADEMIC REPRINTS

The following titles have been reprinted at the request of the
Library Association, and can be obtained from
Cedric Chivers Ltd., Portway, Bath.

Andrews, Kevin	The Flight of Ikaros
Balzac, Honoré de	The Curé de Tours
Broke-Smith, P.W.L.	The History of Early British Military Aeronautics
Cameron, A.	Chemistry in relation to fire risk and extinction
Crozier, F.P.	A Brass Hat in No Man's Land
Crozier, F.P.	The Men I killed
Denham, Jordan	Annals of a Fishing Village
Dewey, John	Interest and Effort in Education
Duncan-Jones, A.	Butler's Moral Philosophy
Ferrier, Susan	Destiny (2 vols.)
Froebel, Friedrich	Education of Man
Galt, John	The Provost
Gates, H.L.	The Auction of Souls
Gilbert, Edmund W.	Brighton Old Ocean's Bauble
Hartley, Dorothy	Thomas Tusser - His good Points of Husbandry
Hawkins, Doris M.	Atlantic Torpedo
Howard, G.E.	Early English Drug Jars
Hughes, A.M.D.	Tennyson Poems published in 1842
Hunt, Henry	Memoirs of Henry Hunt (3 vols.)
Kincaid, Captain J.	Adventures in the Rifle Brigade
Lamb, Harold	Genghis Khan
Lewis, Professor M.M.	Infant Speech
Lewis, R.A.	Edwin Chadwick and the Public Health Movement
Lindsay, Philip	On some Bones in Westminster Abbey
Ling, Princess Der	Imperial Incense
Markham, Sir C.R.	Richard III
Marr. J.E.	The Geology of the Lake District
Martin, Bernard	Strange Vigour

The Institute of Biology's Studies in Biology no. 158

Animal Hormones

John W. Buckle

B.Sc. (Hons) (Sheff.), Ph.D. (Cantab.)
Smith and Nephew Ltd.,
Hull

Edward Arnold

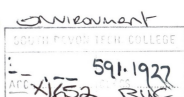

First published in Great Britain 1983
by Edward Arnold (Publishers) Ltd
41 Bedford Square, London WC1B 3DQ

Edward Arnold (Australia) Pty Ltd
80 Waverley Road
Caulfield East 3145
PO Box 234
Melbourne

First Published in United States of America 1983
By Edward Arnold
300 North Charles Street
Baltimore
Maryland 21201

British Library Cataloguing in Publication Data

Buckle, John W.
   Animal hormones.—(The Institute of
   Biology's studies in biology, ISSN 0537-9024; no. 158)
   1. Hormones
   I. Title   II. Series
   591.19'27   QP571

ISBN 0-7131-2874-7

Text set in 9/11 Times Roman
by Castlefield Press, Moulton, Northampton
Printed and bound in Great Britain at
The Camelot Press Ltd, Southampton

General Preface to the Series

Because it is no longer possible for one textbook to cover the whole field of biology while remaining sufficiently up to date, the Institute of Biology proposed this series so that teachers and students can learn about significant developments. The enthusiastic acceptance of 'Studies in Biology' shows that the books are providing authoritative views of biological topics.

The features of the series include the attention given to methods, the selected list of books for further reading and, wherever possible, suggestions for practical work.

Readers' comments will be welcomed by the Education Officer of the Institute.

1983   Institute of Biology
                                                       20 Queensberry Place
                                                       London SW7 2DZ

Preface

Hormones are almost universally distributed throughout the animal kingdom from the primitive organisms such as flatworms to highly sophisticated species including the mammals. They are the chemical messengers that act together with the nervous system to co-ordinate functions as diverse as ionic balance and reproduction, metabolism and immunity, and seasonal colour changes.

This book is designed to act as a general introduction to the study of the hormones and is aimed primarily at sixth form and first year university students. A basic understanding of Biology is assumed. The introductory chapter describes many of the general techniques that have been applied to the study of hormones, and specific methods have been covered where relevant in the later chapters. The first chapter also describes the general principles of hormone action. The remaining chapters are arranged in a manner that should make it easy to dip into the book for reference information.

I am grateful to the many students and colleagues who urged me to write this book. I am also indebted to Sarah Wheeler for translating my rough sketches into the excellent illustrations and to Helen Smith for her faultless care with the manuscript.

Beverley, 1983   J.W.B.

Contents

1 An Introduction to Hormones

During the course of evolution individual cells joined together both anatomically and functionally to form multicellular organisms. With the increase in size and complexity it became increasingly necessary to evolve mechanisms to enable the cells to communicate with one another. The systems that evolved were the nervous system and the hormone (endocrine) system. These two systems do not work in isolation; each interacts with the other in regulating bodily functions.

To ensure that all parts of a multicellular organism function optimally it is important to maintain very fine control over the body's internal environment. For example a small change in the acidity of the blood will render many enzymes almost inactive. The amount of energy needed to maintain a constant blood pH is small in comparison to the amount of energy that would be wasted by running inefficient enzyme systems at an inappropriate pH.

Although the French physiologist Claude Bernard (1813–1875) did not appreciate any of the modern notions of biology, the general principle of a need to maintain internal stability led him to talk of the *milieu interieur* (internal environment) of the body. He realized how important it was to maintain this as constant as possible. This concept is known as homeostasis (Greek: homeo = same, stasis = constant).

However, we must remember that different cells in the body have different optima of pH, temperature, ionic composition, etc. Also their metabolic needs vary from one to another and indeed vary minute by minute. Consequently there is the need for co-ordination of the so-called body compartments. The means of communication within and between compartments is by the endocrine and nervous systems. In view of the interactions between the two systems mentioned above any description of the endocrine system must include some basic understanding of the nervous system. This will be included wherever it is relevant.

During the course of vertebrate evolution there have been few major changes in the positions of the endocrine structures within the body. The endocrine glands will therefore be considered according to the basic mammalian model – the rat. Indeed, much of the experimental work has been based on studies of this animal. Some variants on the rodent theme will be considered since a study of the similarities and differences between species sometimes makes it possible to throw some light upon basic physiological mechanisms.

1.1 What is a hormone?

Many definitions have been used to try to give a succinct and clearcut description of a hormone. Most of these definitions have a number of points in common. Briefly a hormone should fulfil most of the following criteria:

(1) It should be secreted by living cells.

(2) It should be produced in small quantities.

(3) Secretion should be merocrine in nature, i.e. by exocytosis without involving damage to the whole cell.

(4) It should be produced from a ductless gland and be secreted directly into the blood stream.

(5) It should act at specific sites (the so-called 'target organs').

(6) It should regulate (not initiate) the activity of the target organ, eliciting an appropriate response.

(7) It should not be used as a source of energy.

This list may seem unnecessarily exhaustive, however, it does serve to differentiate hormones from enzymes and vitamins and from metabolites such as sugars and fats.

There are numerous other substances that some scientists would consider to be hormones. These include the very important locally-active 'hormones' such as prostaglandins, kinins and wound hormones, and also the neurohormones. Pheromones, the extracorporal social hormones, might also be added to the list. Some of these substances are not covered fully by the definitions above and the working set of criteria must not be considered too restrictive. This book is concerned mainly with vertebrate hormones and only a short chapter considers invertebrate hormones. Interested readers are referred to a specialist text for further insight into this fascinating subject.

1-2 Methods of studying hormones

1.2.1 Extirpation and re-implantation

The basic approach to studying hormones is that of extirpation (i.e. surgical removal) and re-implantation. If a particular gland is thought to produce a hormone it is surgically removed and the effect on the animal observed. Since all endocrine glands have a good blood supply, re-implantation of the gland to a well vascularized area of the body can lead to a resumption of at least part of its former function. Re-implantation sites that have been popular in the past have included the area beneath the thin capsule covering the kidney and in the anterior chamber of the eye. The latter has the advantage of allowing visual inspection of the transplant without further surgical intervention. Obviously this technique is crude and has many criticisms. Nevertheless it has provided some sound endocrinological data.

1.2.2 Extracts

An extension of the basic method described above is to make an extract of the suspect gland and to see if this will correct the malfunction induced by surgical removal of the gland. This extremely important procedure has led to the chemical isolation and subsequent manufacture of many hormones. Synthetic hormones have made it possible to unraval some of the subtleties of endocrinology.

In many cases the extracts of glands have been found to contain several entities and this has led to the discovery of glands with multiple endocrine functions. The pituitary gland, for example, produces no less than nine definite hormones and perhaps several others in some species. However, caution must be used when interpreting the results of such studies since unphysiologically high doses of the extracts may produce effects which are not of biological significance. Consequently the demonstration of appropriate amounts of the hormone in the blood is often necessary before a certain endocrine function is accepted. The amounts of hormone should vary according to physiological stimuli, whether these stimuli be experimentally induced or whether they occur naturally.

1.2.3 Assays

It is always desirable to base assay techniques to measure hormone concentrations on either functional or structural changes that can be measured objectively by instruments rather than relying on subjective assessments. Assays should be based upon normal physiological actions rather than pharmacological effects caused by abnormally large quantities of the substance being evaluated.

One of the earliest methods for assessing the quantity of a hormone present in blood or an extract was the bioassay. This uses the sound principle that the effect of the hormone is directly proportional to the amount of hormone present. An assay of growth hormone – a hormone produced by the pituitary gland – provides a suitable example. The amount of growth is a direct measure of the amount of growth hormone present. This sounds easy in principle. However in practice it is necessary to hypophysectomize the animal, i.e. remove the pituitary gland, to ensure that there is no endogenous (natural) growth hormone present. Animals will not survive this assault unless all the other hormones normally produced by the gland are subsequently replaced. Of course only young animals can be used since the end-point of the assay will be a measure of growth. Also the effects of other factors or hormones influencing growth need to be minimized or eliminated.

What then if a hormone *only* works in the presence of other substances or if its action varies according to the night/day cycle, or the sex of the animal? The problems in setting up such an assay are enormous but not insurmountable. Once these limitations are appreciated and minimized the bioassay can be used.

Numerous similar animals, of the same sex, usually female, are each injected with one of a range of known amounts of pure growth hormone or with the unknown substance. After several days the animals are put down and the width of the epiphyseal cartilages on the tibias measured. Comparison of the unknown with the range of standards gives a quantitative measure of the growth hormone content of the sample.

This method is obviously protracted and indeed the above description leaves out many details and further precautions. Nevertheless bioassays both *in vivo* as above or *in vitro* (i.e. in isolated tissues) have provided useful data on blood and tissue concentrations of hormones under various conditions. Other examples of bioassays include the measurement of blood glucose as the end-point in insulin assays changes in the thyroid gland as an index of thyrotrophin (TSH) activity and the growth of the gonads as a quantitative measure of various reproductive hormones.

The major problem with bioassays, however, is their insensitivity. Relatively large quantities of purified hormone extract are required for each measurement which must then be performed many times to ensure its validity. Other assay methods have therefore been developed which are more sensitive than bioassays.

Chemical assays have been used for some hormones. Probably the most useful has been the determination of protein bound iodine (PBI). This is proportional to the amount of thyroid hormone present, and is still used clinically. However, the general, chemical assays of hormones are rarely used now.

As so often is the case in the biological sciences further rapid expansion awaits the appropriate technical development. The development of saturation analysis, i.e. competitive protein-binding assays and radio immunoassays (RIA), are a case in point. The general principles of these assays are similar:

Pure hormone is mixed with a very small amount of radioactive hormone and an equilibrium is established. A binding agent is added which reacts equally well with both 'labelled' and 'unlabelled' hormone. The bound and unbound hormones are separated from one another and the quantity of radioactivity present in each fraction is measured. The labelled and unlabelled fractions are in equilibrium, therefore if the unlabelled, i.e. endogenous, hormone is in excess, then less of the labelled hormone will be bound when the radioactivity is 'counted'. A series of standards of known hormone concentrations assayed together with the unknowns enables the experimenter to produce a standard curve and so makes it possible to determine the amount of hormone present in a given sample. The general principle is illustrated by Fig. 1-1.

In competitive protein-binding assays the binding is by means of large protein molecules that are non-specific. This means that the sample containing the unknown quantity of the hormone must be fairly pure and elaborate purification procedures are often necessary. However in RIAs an immunoglobulin (antibody) is produced which specifically binds to the hormone concerned. The technicalities of the raising of antibodies are complex and will not be considered here. However, the result is a very specific binding of the hormone that allows the separation and assay of very small quantities of hormones. Nevertheless some preliminary purification of samples is often required since it is not yet possible to raise absolutely pure and specific antibodies.

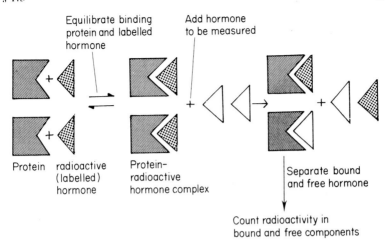

Equilibrate binding
protein and labelled
hormone

Add hormone
to be measured

Protein   radioactive
          (labelled)
          hormone

Protein–
radioactive
hormone complex

Separate bound
and free hormone

Count radioactivity in
bound and free components

Fig. 1-1 General principle of saturation analysis. A known quantity of pure radioactively-labelled hormone is incubated with the sample to be measured. Measurement of radioactivity in the bound or free compartments gives a measure of the amount of hormone in the sample.

It must be appreciated that RIAs can only determine the immunological properties of the hormone and this is not always the same as biological efficacy. A more recent advance has therefore been the development of receptor assays which use specific tissue receptors as the means of binding the hormone and these may give a more physiological measure of hormone concentration. However the extreme accuracy and sensitivity of RIAs when used correctly has led to the processing of many hundreds of hormone samples with concentrations as low as 1 pg ml^{-1} (10^{-12} g ml^{-1}) in a single working day. This has opened up many avenues of hormone research.

1.3 How hormones work

With a few exceptions hormones can be divided into two main groups on the basis of their chemical structure. These are the steroid group and the amines and peptides. Endocrine glands of mesodermal origin use steroids as messengers whereas those of endo- or ectodermal origin use amines and peptides.

The first group of hormones is that containing the amines and peptides. Examples of hormones in this group are insulin, thyroid stimulating hormone (TSH) and luteinizing hormone (LH). The hormones in this group generally bring about their actions within a few minutes and the actions are of only short duration. For example the effect of insulin on blood glucose is very rapid, but only lasts a short while. In general hormones in this group are often stored temporarily within endocrine cells and so are readily available for immediate secretion.

The amines and peptide hormones attach themselves to specific receptors on the cell surface, but they do not enter the cell. The receptor is associated with an enzyme called adenyl cyclase. The hormone-receptor complex activates the adenyl cyclase and causes the breakdown of adenosine triphosphate (ATP) to liberate cyclic adenosine monophosphate (cyclic AMP). The cyclic AMP acts through a complex chain of events causing activation of enzymes. The enzymes

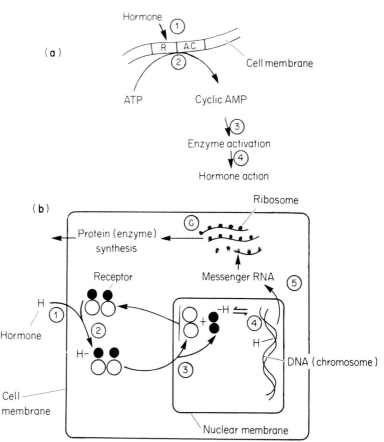

Fig. 1.2 Mechanisms of hormone action. (**a**) **Amines and peptides**. (1) The hormone binds to a receptor (R) on the membrane which activates the adenyl cyclase enzyme (AC); (2) AC converts ATP to cyclic AMP; (3) cyclic AMP activates enzymes by phosphorylation; (4) The activated enzymes bring about the hormone action. (**b**) **Steroids**. (1) The hormone enters the cell and binds to a carrier protein; (2) The carrier transports the hormone to the nucleus; (3) The receptor is liberated to be re-used; (4) The hormone reversibly interacts with the DNA of the chromosone; (5) It activates genes and produces messenger RNA (mRNA); (6) The mRNA passes out of the chromosone and initiates protein (usually enzyme) synthesis on the ribosomes. The enzyme brings about the hormone action.

then bring about the action of the hormone, e.g. the breakdown of fat. The hormone is sometimes described as the body's first messenger and cyclic AMP as the second messenger (Fig. 1-2).

Some hormones elevate cyclic AMP levels and others reduce cyclic AMP production. Clearly if many hormones use a similar intermediate then there must be separation of the chain of events for one hormone from that of another hormone. If there is no compartmentalization, all hormones raising cyclic AMP levels would have the same effect within a cell. There does indeed appear to be such compartmentalization within cells.

The names of many steroid hormones (Fig. 1-3) give an indication that they are steroids – for example progesterone, cortisol, hydrocortisone and oestriol. These hormones have many diverse effects but in general their actions are prolonged, for example in the long term responses to stress or in reproductive development. Thyroxine (T4) and tri-iodothyronine (T3) although chemically unrelated to steroids have a similar cellular mechanism of action and so can be included in this group.

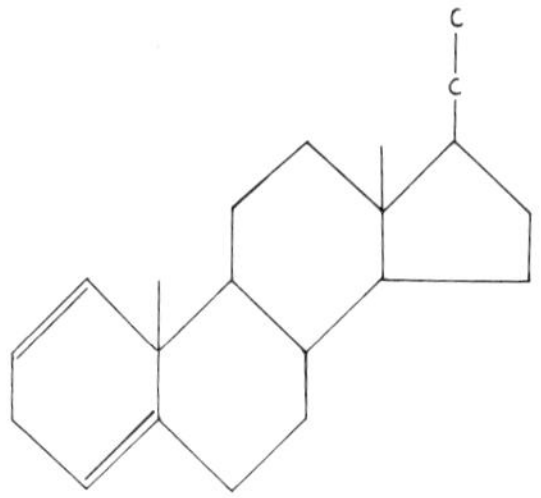

Fig. 1-3   Basic steroid skeleton.

The steroid hormones and T3 and T4 are relatively small molecules and can freely enter cells. Studies with radioactively-labelled hormones have shown that specific carriers transport the hormones across the cytoplasm towards the nucleus. Here the hormone reacts reversibly with DNA, instructing the DNA to initiate protein (enzyme) synthesis (Fig. 1-2). It is probable that the hormone somehow 'switches on' a specific gene or group of genes. When a gene is 'switched on' part of the DNA of one of the chromosomes is decoded in the form of messenger RNA (mRNA). The mRNA passes out of the nucleus to the ribosomes where it initiates protein synthesis. Unlike the amines and peptides which activate enzymes, the steroid hormones initiate the manufacture of new enzymes which are available for fairly long term use.

These general mechanisms are not the only ways in which hormones bring about their effects, and other actions specific to particular hormones will be covered in the relevant chapters.

1.4 Feedback control

An obvious question that arises is how is the effect of a hormone switched off once it has been initiated? The general concept of feedback control is known to all of us in our everyday life, though it is probably not normally so-described. For example, when reaching out to pick up an object our eyes and brain judge the distance and instruct our arm and hand to reach for the object. If we have judged inaccurately and we have over-reached then our hand may touch the object. Nerve impulses are sent back to the brain which responds by a series of countermands to prevent the arm extending further. In other words a message from our hand has fed back to give a negative or cancelling command to the brain. This is known as negative feedback. Similarly when filling a glass with water we pour until we reach the desired level and then negative feedback tells us to stop pouring. Negative feedback is used to a considerable extent in engineering control systems.

Negative feedback exists to control the secretion and release of many hormones and can exert its effect at several levels in the chain of commands. This is illustrated in Fig. 1-4. It is evident that the number of different levels of feedback is considerable. Several different feedbacks may operate simultaneously. It can be seen from the figure that either hormones or the products of hormone activity, for example Ca^{2+} ions or glucose or heat, can feedback negatively to inhibit hormonal release. Further feedbacks may occur higher in the chain. The whole system is called an axis, for example Chapter 2 is concerned principally with the hypothalamic hypophyseal axis, i.e. the links between part of the brain and the pituitary gland.

Often there are at least two hormones controlling a specific function. For example insulin and glucagon regulate blood sugar concentrations. Insulin reduces blood sugar whilst glucagon is antagonistic and increases blood sugar. At any one time the net result is a balance between the actions of the two hormones.

There are also fine controls on the amount of each hormone present. Enzymes in the blood break down the hormones ensuring that they do not persist longer than is necessary. Indeed the so-called half-life (time required for half of the hormone to be broken down) of many hormones is only a matter of a few minutes. In addition at the cellular level prostaglandins may regulate the duration of action of hormones, though details are still unclear.

1.5 Synergism, enhancement and facilitation

One important feature of the action of some hormones is that of *synergism*. This can be explained by a simple hypothetical experimental observation. Hormone 1 causes one unit increase in weight of a gland and hormone 2 causes the same increment in weight. However, when the two hormones are given together the combined effect on growth is greater than the effect predicted by the action of two hormones when given alone. In this example there may be an increase in weight of 10 units. This is called synergism – the combined effect of

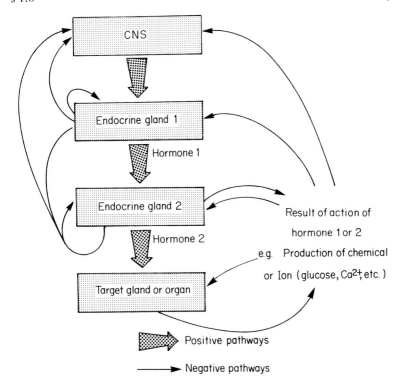

Fig. 1-4 Diagrammatic representation of 'typical' feedback control of an endocrine axis.

the two agents is greater than the arithmetic mean of the effect of the two agents when used alone. Growth hormone often acts synergistically with other hormones.

Synergism should not be confused with *enhancement*. This is where one hormone acts only slightly alone but it greatly enhances the action of another agent. Some hormones show *facilitation*. Here one hormone has no effect alone on a particular system but it enables another hormone to act normally. For example thyroxine (T4) has facilitative actions on the hormones responsible for growth.

1.6 Summary

Hormones are blood-borne messengers that co-ordinate and regulate the actions of different parts of an organism. They are produced in small quantities from ductless glands and affect specific targets. Hormones may be studied by extirpation and re-implantation, by the preparation of extracts or by direct assay methods. In general the polypeptide hormones act rapidly via the so-called 'second messenger' cyclic AMP mechanism causing enzyme activation whilst the steroids act directly on the nucleus of cells initiating protein (enzyme) synthesis. Steroid hormone action is therefore much slower to be initiated but is usually longer lasting. There are elaborate feedback controls both within and between cells and organs to regulate the secretion and breakdown of hormones, so allowing constant regulation of their actions. Hormones often interact with other hormones either by synergism, enhancement or facilitation.

2 Neurosecretion and the Neurohormones

A considerable amount of the early work on neuroendocrinology (the relationship between the endocrine and nervous systems) was directed towards understanding the factors involved with the neural control of the pituitary gland. The great volume of experimental evidence on this system makes it a suitable place to introduce the concept of neurosecretion. However, it is very important to realize that the nervous and endocrine systems are juxtaposed at many sites in the body; not only do nerves influence hormonal activity but hormones affect nervous activity also. This chapter explores some of the interactions between the nervous and endocrine systems and examines how the pituitary gland and the brain intercommunicate.

2.1 Neurosecretion

When a nerve impulse passes along a neuron (nerve cell) it brings about changes in the electrical charge between the inside and the outside of the neuronal cell membrane. These electrical changes, called the action potential, pass along the neuron and so transmit messages from one area of the body to another. However, action potentials cannot cross synapses, the junctions between neurons. At the synapses a chemical neurotransmitter is liberated. The transmitter traverses the short synaptic cleft and at the post-synaptic membrane it causes a new nerve impulse to be generated. Several neurotransmitters are known to exist, but the most widely spread are adrenalin, noradrenalin and acetylcholine.

Nervous activity is very specific, each series of nerve impulses eliciting a particular response. Often this is a considerable advantage, allowing a localized response to be produced. However, if a more generalized effect is required then a whole series of nerve impulses needs to be elicited, one to each gland that is to respond. This is very expensive in terms of energy.

During the course of evolution some nerve endings have developed the ability to release their neurotransmitter directly into the circulation where it exerts a more general effect. An example of this is the adrenal medulla which is composed of specialized nervous tissue. One of the products of the adrenal gland, adrenalin acts by targeting a number of well defined sites in the body (see Chapter 5). Adrenalin is produced from a neuron yet it equally has many of the characteristics of a hormone. Thus the concept of neurosecretion has arisen. Neurosecretion enables the nervous system to regulate endocrine activity. Figure 2-1 illustrates the similarities and differences between neurotransmission and neurosecretion. The remainder of this chapter will

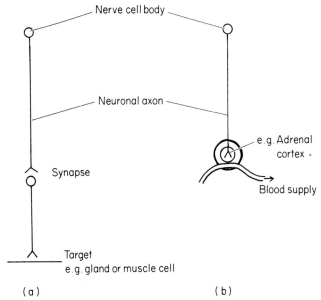

Fig. 2-1 (a) Neurotransmission and (b) neurosecretion. A neurotransmitter is liberated from a nerve ending and passes across a synapse to activate another neuron. In neurosecretion the transmitter is released directly into the blood stream.

consider the hypothalamic–hypophyseal axis to illustrate some aspects of neurosecretion.

2.2 The hypothalamic–hypophyseal axis

There is some confusion over the nomenclature of parts of the pituitary gland. Traditionally the structures are described on the basis of their anatomical position in man. For example the anterior lobe is at the front and the posterior lobe at the back, with the intermediate lobe between the two. The pituitary stalk connects the gland to the brain. However, there has been a shift in emphasis in recent years and structures are now more commonly named on the basis of their function rather than on their anatomical location. The term hypophysis is used for the pituitary gland and the anterior lobe becomes the adenohypophysis (Greek: aden = glandular), the posterior lobe becomes the neurohypophysis because of its neural origin and so on. Both sets of names and several other alternatives are shown in Fig. 2-2.

In this book the more modern functionally-related names will be used since the simpler anatomical names belie the fact that the anatomy of different species varies. In some fish, for example, the intermediate lobe is not between the other two lobes, and indeed in some species the intermediate lobe is not anatomically discrete.

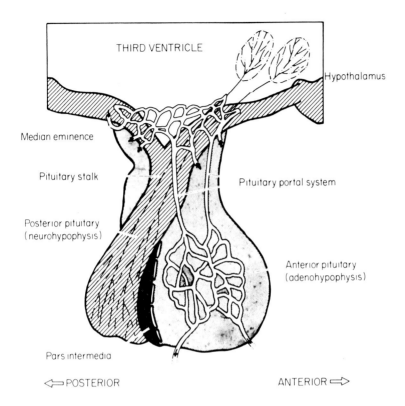

THIRD VENTRICLE

Hypothalamus

Median eminence

Pituitary stalk

Pituitary portal system

Posterior pituitary
(neurohypophysis)

Anterior pituitary
(adenohypophysis)

Pars intermedia

⇐ POSTERIOR   ANTERIOR ⇒

Fig. 2-2 The pituitary gland. The various names for the component parts are indicated.

Embryologically the pituitary gland has a dual origin. The adenohypophysis arises from an upgrowth of the roof of the mouth (stomodeum), whilst the neurohypophysis develops as a downgrowth from the infundibulum, an outpocketing of part of the brain called the hypothalamus (Fig. 2-3). The resultant structure weighs only 500 mg in man and is surrounded by bone. It remains in neural contact with the brain and a vascular link also develops. These two links are vital for the brain's control over the endocrine function of the pituitary gland. The adenohypophysis and the neurohypophysis are anatomically very closely associated. However, functionally the two glands are discrete entities.

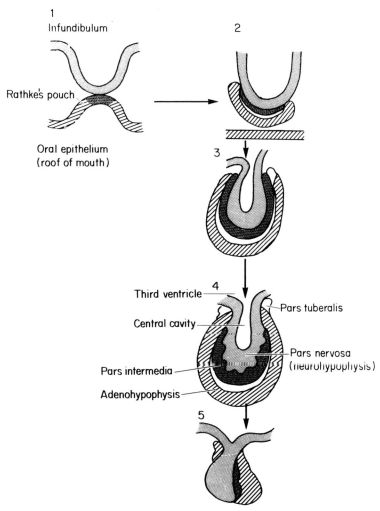

Fig. 2-3 The embryological development of the pituitary gland from a downgrowth of the hypothalamus and an upgrowth of the roof of the mouth.

2.3 The neurohypophysis (posterior pituitary gland)

The neurohypophysis develops embryologically from the hypothalamus. This area is known to control many functions including body temperature, sleep, wakefulness, drinking and eating. After development the hypothalamus maintains its link with the neurohypophysis and so the control of the pituitary gland can be added to the list of hypothalamic functions outlined above.

There is evidence for two hormones being produced from the neurohypophysis. These are oxytoxin and antidiuretic hormone (ADH) – sometimes called vasopressin. The two hormones are similar chemically, each consisting of eight amino acids, and each has an effective circulatory half-life of two to four minutes due to rapid enzymatic degradation.

2.3.1 Antidiuretic hormone

Removal of the neurohypophysis causes a transient diabetes insipidis (not to be confused with diabetes mellitus – sugar diabetes) where the urine flow increases enormously and very dilute urine is produced. This experiment and others have demonstrated the presence of a hormone from the neurohypophysis that is antidiuretic, i.e. it prevents the excretion of dilute urine. In order to indentify the site of action of the hormone, purified extracts of ADH 'labelled' with radioactivity or with a fluorescent marker have been injected into animals. Subsequent microscopic examination has demonstrated the presence of the marker principally in the distal convoluted tubules (DCTs) and collecting ducts of the kidney. This observation ties in well with the known role of the DCTs and collecting ducts in modifying water re-absorption. However, ADH probably has other effects on water balance – for example it may increase or decrease the water content of muscle cells.

The main stimulus for ADH secretion is a rise in plasma osmolality, i.e. concentration. There are specialized osmoreceptor cells in the hypothalamus that seem to react to this change. For example drinking a lot of water will decrease ADH release so allowing a diuresis to occur to ensure the blood volume does not rise excessively. A salty meal has the reverse effect and the hypothalamic cells stimulate ADH release, limiting diuresis and so conserving water. In this situation if water were not conserved the plasma osmolality would rise and might cause cellular damage.

The links between the hypothalamus and the neurohypophysis which bring about these changes have only been discovered in the last 20 years. The observation that ablation (removal) of the neurohypophysis causes only a transient and reversible diuresis gave some clues indicating that the neurohypophysis itself is not essential. Indeed following the return to 'normal' after such a neurohypophysectomy blood ADH levels within the normal range have been observed.

ADH is now known to be manufactured in the hypothalamus, and it has been possible to localize the site of ADH production using elaborate electrophysiological techniques to record from and stimulate neurons in specific areas of the brain. ADH is transported along nerve axons to the neurohypophysis by an ill-understood mechanism called axonal flow. It is stored in the neurohypophysis until required, and can be released at very short notice. Ablation of the gland causes ADH to be released at the cut nerve endings of the pituitary stalk, so reversing the experimental diabetes insipidis.

In addition to the osmoreceptor modulation of ADH release, volume receptors in the atria of the heart send messages via the vagus nerve (Xth

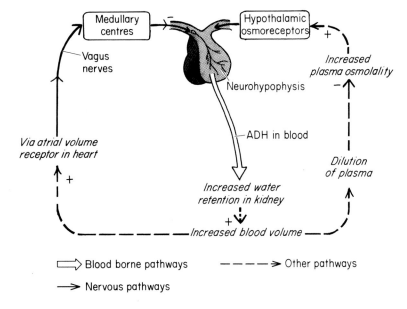

Fig. 2-4   Schematic representation of the principal actions of ADH.

cranial nerve) to regulate the activity of the cells producing ADH. Details of this pathway are shown in Fig. 2-4.

2.3.2 Oxytocin

Oxytocin, like ADH, is an octapeptide produced in the hypothalamus and stored in the neurohypophysis. It causes contractions of the myoepithelial cells found in females in the milk ducts of the breast and in the uterine myometrium.

When a baby suckles at the nipple nerve impulses pass along the spinal cord to the hypothalamus and oxytocin release is stimulated. Oxytocin is carried via the blood stream to the capillaries supplying the milk ducts. Here oxytocin causes contraction of the myoepithelial cells. The arrangement of the cells around the milk ducts causes them to squeeze milk along the ducts when the cells contract and so milk is available to the feeding infant. This release of milk (milk 'let down') on demand is a reflex action (Fergussen's Reflex, Fig. 2-5) controlled by the suckling stimulus. Milk continues to be released until the milk ducts are empty or until the suckling stops. The emptying of the milk ducts is *one* of the stimuli for further milk production (lactogenesis). This is discussed later (Chapter 7).

Oxytocin plays a role in the regulation of uterine contractions where again it affects involuntary (smooth) muscle cells. Its role is principally at the end of

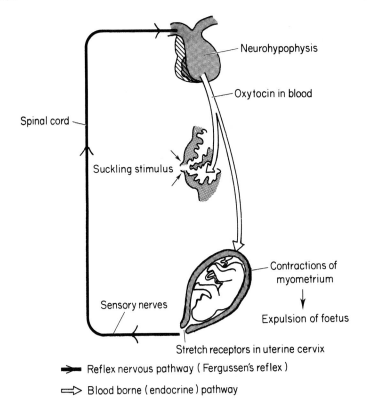

Reflex nervous pathway (Fergussen's reflex)

Blood borne (endocrine) pathway

Fig. 2-5 Schematic representation of the principal actions of oxytocin.

pregnancy where it is one of the many hormones controlling the myometrial contractions of labour. Further details are discussed in the chapter on female reproduction (Chapter 7). Oxytocin's role in males, if any, awaits clarification.

2.4 Summary

The release of hormones from modified nerve endings is known as neurosecretion, and is one of the ways in which endocrine function is regulated by the nervous system. Antidiuretic hormone (ADH) and oxytocin are octapeptide hormones produced in the hypothalamus and stored in the neurohypophysis. Both hormones act rapidly and have a short half-life enabling rapid and controlled responses to stimuli. ADH is concerned with water regulation and acts at the renal distal convoluted tubules and collecting ducts. Oxytocin controls milk 'let down' and uterine contractions in females.

3 The Adenohypophysis and Hypothalamus

3.1 Hypothalamic control of the adenohypophysis

The pituitary gland has often been described as the 'master gland' or the 'conductor of the endocrine orchestra' where it is said to control many of the other endocrine systems in the body. However, it is now known that the hypothalamus, a small portion of the forebrain directly above the pituitary gland, produces its own hormones which themselves control the release and/or manufacture of the adenohypophyseal hormones.

Some of the earliest evidence for the hypothalamic control of the adenohypophysis comes from the work of a famous Oxford physiologist G.W. Harris in the 1940s and 50s. He studied the blood supply connecting the two tissues. This is a portal system and is analogous to the other portal system in the body, the hepatic portal vein. Both consist of veins which connect one capillary network (or plexus) to a secondary plexus. In the hypothalamic–hypophyseal portal system blood from the primary plexus in the hypothalamus drains through the portal veins into a secondary plexus which runs over the adenohypophysis before draining into the venous system (Fig. 2-2). This allows the hypothalamic hormones to act on the pituitary gland without having systemic effects.

In man there is no pituitary artery and all the blood to the adenohypophysis comes via the portal system, though in most animals there is also a direct blood supply to the pituitary gland. G.W. Harris was the first to observe that the blood flowed from the hypothalamus to the adenohypophysis, and this suggested that the brain could regulate adenohypophyseal function.

Further experimental evidence for the role of the portal system has come from very sophisticated experiments where the minute quantities of blood from the portal system were collected and assayed. Also studies involving the micro-injection of extracts of the hypothalamus into parts of the pituitary gland have helped explain the complex interrelationships between the pituitary and the hypothalamus.

In the early experiments blood-borne factors were detected, and these were found to stimulate the release of the adenohypophyseal hormones. These substances were called releasing factors or releasing hormones. However, it now appears that each adenohypophyseal hormone has its own release-inhibiting hormone as well as its own releasing hormone, so the picture has become much more complex. With the exception of prolactin the releasing function is dominant over the inhibiting factor under normal conditions. It is usual to abbreviate the names of the hormones from the pituitary gland and abbreviations are also used for the releasing and releasing-inhibiting hormones. Growth hormone releasing hormone and growth hormone release inhibiting hormone are known as GHRH and GHRIH (or GHIH) respectively.

Many of the techniques described in Chapter 1 have been used to clarify the endocrine function of the hypothalamus and adenohypophysis. In addition, correlating changes in the histology of the adenohypophysis with different physiological states has proved useful. However, this approach must only be used with caution since cells may be depleted of hormones because they are either very active or because they are inactive. An active cell may be manufacturing a hormone at its maximum rate and the hormone is secreted almost immediately due to the demand. Therefore there will be no hormone stores in the cell. An inactive cell may not have any stored hormone since it may only be manufactured on demand. Therefore extreme care must be exercised in the interpretation of such histological changes and trying to correlate them with physiological changes. However, the use of electron microscopy has made it easier to study the parts of the cell responsible for hormone biosynthesis and has helped to clarify some of the relationships between structure and function.

One other useful technique that has been particularly useful in the study of pituitary function has been to study patients with known defects in pituitary function. For example a pituitary tumour can cause acromegaly or gigantism due to excessive growth hormone (GH) secretion, or dwarfism due to inadequate GH secretion.

3.2 The adenohypophyseal hormones

All of the hormones produced from the adenohypophysis are polypeptides and chemically they have a lot of features in common. Four of the six hormones are described as trophic hormones (from the Greek meaning to feed), i.e. they control the basal activity of other glands. These hormones are ACTH, TSH, FSH, and LH (Fig. 3-1). They will be considered first.

3.2.1 ACTH

Adrenocorticotrophic hormone (ACTH, adrenocorticotrophin, cortico-trophin) is a single chain polypeptide of 39 amino acids. It was first clearly shown to exist in 1927. The function of ACTH is to control the adrenal gland. Like many of the pituitary polypeptides biological activity of the hormone only requires some of the amino acid residues to be present (in this case the first 20 are essential). It is not known what the other amino acids are for but one suggestion is that they delay the breakdown of the hormone in the circulation and so prolong its action. Despite this ACTH has a half-life of only five to ten minutes. Consequently plasma concentrations can be finely regulated.

ACTH is essential over the long term to initiate and maintain the full functional development of the adrenal gland, and in the absence of ACTH the adrenal cortex atrophies. In the short term it acts very quickly, within seconds to minutes, and its principal action is to stimulate hydrocortisone and corticosterone secretion, with only minimal effects on aldosterone secretion (see Chapter 5). The adrenal responds both to the absolute amount of ACTH

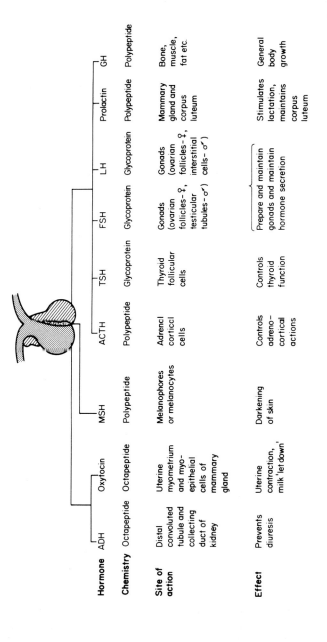

Hormone	ADH	Oxytocin		MSH	ACTH	TSH	FSH	LH	Prolactin	GH
Chemistry	Octapeptide	Octapeptide		Polypeptide	Polypeptide	Glycoprotein	Glycoprotein	Glycoprotein	Polypeptide	Polypeptide
Site of action	Distal convoluted tubule and collecting duct of kidney	Uterine myometrium and myo-epithelial cells of mammary gland		Melanophores or melanocytes	Adrenal cortical cells	Thyroid follicular cells	Gonads (ovarian follicles-♀, testicular tubules-♂)	Gonads (ovarian follicles-♀, interstitial cells-♂)	Mammary gland and corpus luteum	Bone, muscle, fat etc.
Effect	Prevents diuresis	Uterine contraction, milk 'let down'		Darkening of skin	Controls adreno-cortical actions	Controls thyroid function	Prepare and maintain gonads and maintain hormone secretion		Stimulates lactation, maintains corpus luteum	General body growth

Fig. 3-1 The hormones produced by the pituitary gland.

and to a change in the secretion of ACTH; therefore a small increase in ACTH secretion rate will have an effect on the adrenal gland.

Other actions for ACTH have been proposed and these are based on *in vitro* experimentation. The actions which may be of significance are direct effects on the mobilization of adipose tissue and interactions with hydrocortisone. Some of the other actions observed *in vitro* may be due to the similarity in the chemical structure of ACTH and the other pituitary peptides. However, there is good evidence that foetal ACTH plays a role in the initiation of parturition (birth) in some species (see Chapter 7).

3.2.2 TSH

Thryoid stimulating hormone (thyrotrophin) regulates the activity of the thyroid gland, details of which will be covered in Chapter 4. It stimulates growth of the size and number of thyroid follicular cells, as well as stimulating the release of thyroid hormones. In addition to its direct action on the thyroid gland TSH may also increase the uptake of thyroxine (T4) into muscle cells. TSH is a glycoprotein, i.e. a protein with a polysaccharide sugar component. The amino acid sequence is not known but it has a molecular weight of around 30 000 to 36 000. It has a relatively long half-life for a glycoprotein, this being between 35 and 55 minutes in plasma. It is metabolized mainly by the kidney.

3.2.3 FSH and LH

Follicle stimulating hormone and luteinizing hormone are gonadotrophins, i.e. they are directly concerned with regulating the activity of the gonads, the testes and ovaries. For many years it was thought that FSH and LH were chemically identical. Both are glycoproteins and have relatively long half-lives of about 60 minutes.

FSH is concerned mainly with stimulating development of the ovarian follicle (*not* the ovum) in the female – hence its name. In males it is necessary for the development of the testicular tubules and the maintenance and differentiation of spermatozoa. However, it is still known as FSH in human males despite the fact that it does not affect the follicle!

LH is necessary for ovulation and luteinization of the follicle to form the corpus luteum. Luteinization is the process occurring immediately after ovulation where the cells of the follicle invaginate to form a dense corpus luteum ('yellow body') which subsequently secretes progesterone. Some LH is necessary for the actions of FSH on the follicle, so functionally the two hormones are very closely related. In the male, LH is also known as interstitial cell stimulating hormone (ICSH) since it stimulates the development of the Leydig cells (interstitial cells) of the testes and causes them to secrete testosterone. Again FSH enhances this action.

The actions of LH and FSH in males and females are not too dissimilar in principle. FSH is necessary for preparing and maintaining the gonads and for initiating the development of the sex cells. LH is necessary for development of the hormone-producing cells and, with FSH, it maintains the secretion of these hormones. Fuller details of the endocrinology of LH and FSH are to be found in the chapters on male and female reproduction (Chapters 6 and 7 respectively).

3.2.4 Prolactin

Prolactin has been given many names including lactogenic hormone, mammotrophin, lactogen and luteotrophin, and these names underline the confusion about the action of the hormone. The luteotrophic action (i.e. promoting the formation of the corpus luteum) has only been demonstrated in some species, therefore some investigators feel that this term is inappropriate. Similar arguments can be used against the other names. However, prolactin is a term that has the most common usage. In some species there is debate as to whether its actions can be explained on the basis of other hormones, particularly growth hormone. However, in several species prolactin has been definitely shown to be a distinct polypeptide hormone which is chemically similar to growth hormone.

Prolactin is undoubtedly the most versatile of the adenohypophyseal hormones and this versatility defies a single unifying theory to explain the many actions of the hormone. In females it stimulates and maintains lactation, and maintains the corpus luteum causing it to secrete progesterone. This second luteotrophic action is not a property of prolactin in all species, adding to the confusion that has arisen around this hormone. The concept of a luteotrophic complex has been used to explain this. In some species the luteotrophic complex is a mixture of LH, FSH and prolactin whereas in other species only LH and FSH are necessary for normal luteal function. Oestrogens may also be part of the luteotrophic complex in some animals, e.g. the rabbit.

In some species prolactin is involved with such diverse actions as arousing parental behaviour (birds and perhaps rats) stimulating the growth of the crop sac (some birds – this was used as a bioassay for the hormone), stimulation of growth (reptiles) and the drive for water (amphibians). Numerous actions on fat and carbohydrate metabolism have also been shown. In mammals few actions specific to the male have been demonstrated other than perhaps direct stimulation of prostatic growth, possible synergistic actions with testosterone, and a decrease in sexual activity.

Prolactin is unusual in that its control by the hypothalamus is mainly by means of an inhibiting hormone (prolactin release inhibiting hormone, PRIH, PIH), the releasing hormone (PRH) plays a subsidiary role in controlling secretion.

3.2.5 Growth hormone (GH)

GH is sometimes known as somatotrophin or STH. It is a polypeptide of 188 amino acids in man, the structure varying from species to species. It is similar chemically to prolactin and causes general tissue growth without maturation or development. It has many other actions including effects on metabolism which are clearly related to its action on growth. GH does not usually act alone, it can enhance or facilitate the action of other hormones as well as acting in a synergistic manner.

Details of the metabolic effects of growth hormone are given in Chapter 10. It has a plasma half-life of 30 minutes in man, and there is evidence that it is enzymatically degraded in the circulation, being constantly turned over at a rate of about 3% per minute. The tibia bioassay technique that was developed for GH has been described in Chapter 1.

3.3 The intermediate lobe – melanocyte (melanophore) stimulating hormone (MSH)

The intermediate lobe of the pituitary gland is derived from similar tissue to that from which the adenohypophysis develops. It produces one hormone called MSH (melanocyte stimulating hormone in mammals; melanophore stimulating hormone in lower species) or intermedin. MSH is a peptide with two forms, one of 13 amino acids and another of 18 amino acids, and it is closely related chemically to part of the ACTH molecule. These chemical similarities explain some observations such as the MSH-like activity of ACTH in man. MSH, however, has no ACTH-like activity.

MSH has a plasma half-life of about two hours and in fish and amphibians it causes darkening of the pigment cells (chromatophores) by causing them to change shape. When the cells are expanded the animal appears dark and when they are contracted the animal appears lighter in colour. The mechanisms controlling the chromatophores are complex since the melanin-containing cells (melanophores) respond to MSH, to secretions from the pineal gland and also to nervous stimulation. There are also other coloured pigment cells in the skin and the interrelationships between the expansion and contraction of these cells leads to the elaborate patterns used for sexual display and camouflage which appear on the skin of many lower animals.

In mammals a definitive function for MSH has not been identified, though it may play a role in regulating skin pigmentation by stimulating the manufacture of melanin in the melanophores. These pigment cells do not change shape but appear darker or lighter due to the quantity of melanin present. In mammals MSH may also affect nervous tissue excitibility.

3.4 Summary

The manufacture and/or secretion of the adenohypophyseal hormones is under a dual control from the hypothalamus. The release or release-inhibiting hormones travel down the hypothalamic–hypophyseal portal system and the balance between the two hormones regulates the minute-to-minute secretion of the adenohypophyseal hormones. The four trophic hormones produced are ACTH to regulate adrenal cortical activity, TSH to control the thyroid gland and the gonadotrophins FSH and LH to regulate gonadal function. Prolactin has many diverse actions including those on sexual function, and GH controls general body growth. The intermediate lobe of the pituitary produces one hormone MSH and this controls colour changes in lower species, though its function in man is not clear.

The pituitary gland is *not* a master endocrine gland controlling *all* others but it is clearly a very important regulatory centre that plays a major role in bringing together the nervous and endocrine components of the body's co-ordinating system.

4 The Thyroid Gland

The thyroid gland consists of two lobes, one lobe lying on each side of the trachea. There is a thin isthmus running across the trachea and this connects the two lobes of the gland. Thyroid glands are present in the majority of vertebrates but they vary to some extent in shape and anatomical position. In man an enlarged thyroid gland (or goitre) has been known clinically for thousands of years but it was not until the latter years of the last century that an understanding of the hormone deficiency causing the disease became known.

4.1 Anatomy and ultrastructure

In 1656 Thomas Wharton coined the name thyroid ('shield shaped') for the prominent gland found in the neck. In man it weighs between 25 and 40 g, depending on its functional state. Like many endocrine glands it is well vascularized taking its arterial supply direct from the subclavian and internal carotid arteries. It has been calculated that on a weight for weight basis the thyroid gland receives more blood than the kidneys, and is second only to the adrenal gland in the amount of blood flowing through each gram of tissue.

Microscopically the gland is made up of many tens of thousands of follicles (Fig. 4-1). Each follicle consists of a ball of epithelial cells enclosing a cavity which contains an homogenous amber-coloured gelatinous mass of a globulin called thyroglobulin. Thyroglobulin is a colloid that is produced by the secretory epithelium and is the storage product of the gland. The quantity of colloid in each follicle of the gland varies according to the gland's functional state. Surrounding the follicles is a well vascularized network of connective tisssue. In the connective tissue some cells are found which tend to stain less densely than their surroundings and these 'light' cells or parafollicular cells are thought to secrete thyrocalcitonin. Howeyer they have a separate embryological origin from the remainder of the thyroid cells and will be considered in a later section (Chapter 11).

Experimentally it has been shown that when the thyroid gland is active the epithelial cells become low and cuboidal in appearance and the colloid accumulates in the follicles. An inactive gland is often, but not always, characterized by columnar epithelial cells and the colloid is depleted. As has been stated in an earlier chapter, extreme care must be exercised in using histological evidence alone to establish the functional state of a gland.

4.2 Thyroxine and tri-iodothyronine

In 1895 iodine was accidentally discovered in thyroid extracts and it is now

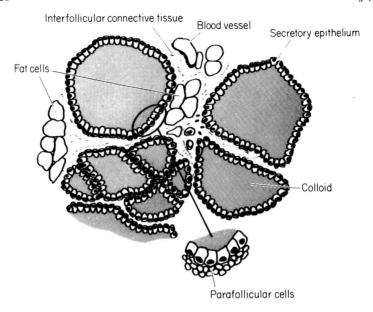

Fat cells

Interfollicular connective tissue

Blood vessel

Secretory epithelium

Colloid

Parafollicular cells

Fig. 4-1 Cross section of the thyroid follicles.

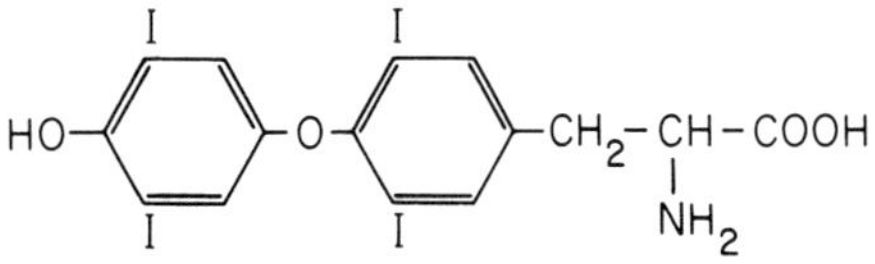

Thyroxine

3,5,3',5'-Tetra-iodothyronine- (T4)

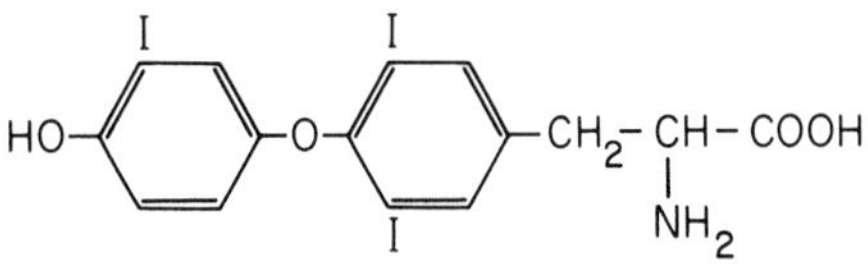

3,5,3'-Tri-iodothyronine-(T3)

Fig. 4-2 Chemical structures of T4 and T3.

known that the thyroid gland is extremely prolific in its ability to concentrate iodine. It is capable of concentrating iodine to over one hundred times the plasma level.

Thyroxine, the main hormone produced from the gland, was first isolated in 1914 but its chemical structure (Fig. 4-2) was not known for a further twelve years. Thyroxine is often known as T4 since it contains four iodine atoms attached to a thyronine nucleus. Soon after T4 was identified it became clear that a second similar component was produced by the thyroid gland and some 25 years later tri-iodothyronine (T3) was isolated and synthesized (Fig. 4-2). Although T3 is up to five times as potent as T4 it is synthesized in smaller amounts. Both hormones have similar actions and are carried in the blood bound to plasma proteins.

Iodine is ingested in small quantities as part of our normal diet. About 70 mg is adequate for the daily intake since the body shows great economy in handling its iodine stores. Most of the iodine freed through the metabolism of the thyroid hormones is retained and is recycled.

The thyroid gland selectively and actively takes up iodine from the plasma. An 'iodine pump' has been located on the outer border of the follicular cells. This 'pump' like many similar mechanisms in living cells involves an ATP-ase (adenosine triphosphatase) enzyme located in a cell membrane. When the substance to be 'pumped' (in this case iodine) against a concentration or electrical gradient binds to one side of the 'pump' the ATP-ase cleaves ATP to produce ADP (adenosine diphosphate) liberating phosphate and energy. The energy is used to modify the membrane, perhaps creating temporary 'pores' which allow iodine through into the follicular cells. Iodine can move in either direction, both into and out of the cell using this mechanism. However, the equilibrium strongly favours uptake. The electron microscope has revealed that the epithelial cells of the follicles have deep folds on their outer surface and numerous microvilli on the inner surface. These folds and microvilli increase the surface area of the cell membranes, a feature often found at sites of membrane transport mechanisms.

Once inside the follicular cells the iodine is oxidized and it is then released into the colloid and can attach to one of the tyrosine amino acids on the thyroglobulin molecule to form mono-iodotyrosine. This is then converted to mono-iodotyramine (MIT) and di-iodotyramine (DIT), the precursors of T3 and T4. Coupling of two DIT molecules produces T4 and the joining of one MIT molecule with one DIT molecule produces T3. The majority of these reactions take place while still attached to the thyroglobulin molecule. The thyroglobulin with T4 and T3 attached is stored as the colloid in the lumen. Finally a protease enzyme is secreted into the lumen by the follicular cells, and this releases T4 and T3 from the thyroglobulin. The process is enhanced by thyroid stimulating hormone (TSH). The folded surface of the membrane between the follicular cell and the lumen provides a large surface across which the enzyme can be released. Much of the evidence for the characterization of these pathways comes from studies using the radioactive isotope ^{131}I as a tracer for iodine.

4.3 The actions of the thyroid hormones

The thyroid hormones have a diversity of actions in both young and mature animals. These actions can be categorized into two general groups: (1) growth-promoting and developmental actions and (2) metabolic actions.

4.3.1 Growth promoting and developmental actions

T4 stimulates general body growth and deficiencies of the hormone can lead to dwarfism. However, many of the actions of T4 and T3 occur in juvenile animals and include stimulation of general growth, maturation and development of many body systems including the central nervous system. A deficiency of the thyroid hormones will retard growth and development, but these actions can be reversed by hormone replacement therapy with T3 or T4 so long as this occurs before too much damage has been done.

The actions of the thyroid hormones on growth and development are demonstrated by a simple series of experiments using amphibians. Exposure of frog or toad tadpoles to water deficient in iodine delays their development, producing giant tadpoles. The addition of iodine or the thyroid hormones to the water leads to the adoption of the adult form; the limbs develop fully, the tail regresses and the adult form is produced. There are some Mexican salamanders which live in high mountain lakes deficient in iodine that were originally only known in their juvenile form in the wild. These axolotls had even developed the ability to reproduce in their juvenile form, i.e. they were neotenous. Members of the same species living in water containing normal quantities of iodine develop into salamanders as normal. Iodine or thyroid hormones have since been shown to cause this metamorphosis.

In mamamals T4 is known to help proper bone development and is essential for full development of the nervous system. Cretinism is a disease causing children to be physically deformed and severely mentally retarded. Some types of cretinism are caused by the inability to couple DIT and/or MIT to produce T4 and T3. If this is recognized early enough and replacement therapy initiated, then the child may not become too badly deformed and the intelligence may not be too greatly impaired. However, since the nervous system develops during the last months of intra-uterine life and during the first year of life, complete normal development is not always possible since the symptoms of deficiency may not be evident until it is too late. How T4 affects development and maturation of the central nervous system is unknown.

4.3.2 Metabolic actions

Thyroid hormones speed up a number of metabolic processes and enhance or facilitate many others. They have a calorigenic action helping to liberate energy and seem to act on the mitochondria, though exact details are not clear. The thyroid hormones increase carbohydrate, fat and cholesterol metabolism, and some of these actions will be considered in the chapter on metabolism (Chapter 10).

T4 and T3 affect the metabolism of calcium and magnesium and help to regulate the secretion of hydrocortisone from the adrenal gland and GH from the adenohypophysis. Milk production is assisted by the presence of thyroid hormones, this being facilitative action.

In general T4 and T3 increase the basal metabolic rate, so hyperthyroid patients will be very active, with a rapid heart rate, they will lose weight and will be mentally restless. This disease may cause gigantism in the young or 'Graves disease' if it occurs later in life. It is often characterized by an enlarged thyroid gland. Hypothyroidism can also cause the thyroid to enlarge since it is overworking and trying ineffectively to produce enough T4 and T3. 'Derbyshire Neck' is a classic example; people living in a region of Derbyshire deficient in iodine often had a goitre. Cretinism and dwarfism were prevalent amongst juveniles in the area and the mature subjects were fat, had coarse skin, a decreased mental activity and a low basal metabolic rate. These lethargic people suffered from myxoedema, i.e. hypothyroidism.

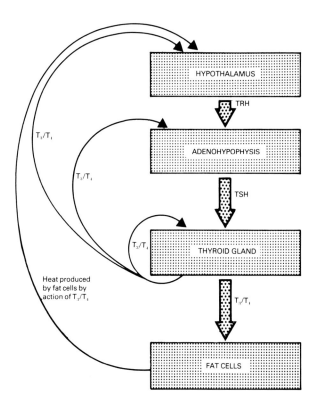

Fig. 4.3   A diagrammatic representation of some of the major feedback controls of the thyroid axis.

4.4   Control of the thyroid axis

The main regulator of thyroid hormone secretion is TSH, though the gland does have some autoregulatory activity. The negative feedback mechanisms described in Chapter 1 affect the thyroid axis. The presence of T4 in the blood decreases TSH secretion from the pituitary and TRH secretion from the hypothalamus. Also a build up of T4 in the thyroid may slow further T4 production, and T4 release may be a factor regulating further synthesis.

In addition to the endocrine feedback mechanisms there may be feedback by other factors. For example cold may increase TSH secretion in some animals and emotional stress and light have been shown to stimulate TSH secretion in other species. It is known that the areas of the hypothalamus controlling temperature and hunger are near the hypothalamic area regulating TRH secretion and many new physiological controls over the thyroid axis may become apparent. The majority of these may offer fine control over the thyroid axis but by far the major regulating factor is TSH (Fig. 4-3).

4.5   Summary

The thyroid gland produces T3 and T4 which have similar actions, though T3 is more potent and acts more rapidly. However considerably more T4 is present in the blood. Both hormones contain iodine and are stored attached to thyroglobulin in the thyroid follicles.

Their actions are to aid development and maturation of the skeletal and central nervous systems and to control growth and metabolic rate. The absence or overproduction of the thyroid hormones leads to clearly defined clinical disorders. The control of thyroid function is principally by TSH but a fine control is exerted by various feedback loops involving thyroid hormones, heat, light, stress and possibly other signals. The majority of these feedbacks occur at the level of the hypothalamus.

5 The Adrenal Gland: Cortex and Medulla

Although the adrenal glands were first described over four hundred years ago by Eustachius, whose name is given to the Eustachian tube of the ear, it was not until some 60 years ago that it became clear that they were composite glands. It had been known that the glands were essential for life but in the 1920s it was discovered that this was not due to the loss of adrenalin but due to the absence of other hormones now known to emanate from the adrenal cortex.

5.1 Anatomy

There are two adrenal glands and each is situated anterior to the kidney. They are usually triangular in shape (Fig. 5-1), and they reach their maximum size relative to the rest of the body in the foetus during the third month of pregnancy. The foetal adrenal clearly plays an important role, though what this role is has yet to be fully clarified. Recent work suggests a role in the termination of pregnancy and in lung development (Chapter 7).

The adrenal glands are each surrounded by a relatively thick capsule and beneath this each gland is clearly divided into two regions, the outer cortex and the medullary core. The cortex has three vaguely defined zones, the zona glomerulosa, zona fasciculata and zona reticularis (Fig. 5-1). The different zones contain different enzyme systems and each produces its own hormones.

The adrenal medulla derives embryologically from the nervous system and

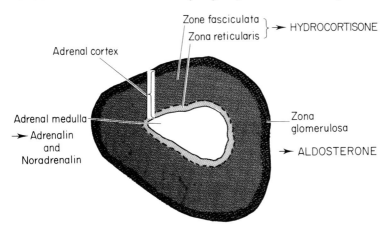

Fig. 5-1 The adrenal gland and its secretions.

the association with the cortical cells becomes more pronounced in the higher vertebrate species. It is likely that the hormones of the adrenal cortex enhance the ability of the medulla to produce these hormones.

5.2 The adrenal cortex

The adrenal cortex produces steroid hormones and these are essential to life. It is the removal of the cortex that will lead to eventual death after bilateral adrenalectomy. Almost fifty different steroids have been isolated from the mammalian adrenal cortex. Many of these are intermediates in the biosynthesis of the active hormones. Two major groups of biologically-active hormones are produced from the cortex. These are the glucocorticoids produced by the zona fasciculata and zona reticularis, and the mineralo-corticoids produced by the outer zona glomerulosa. In addition the gland produces small quantities of the sex steroids, i.e. androgens, oestrogens and progestogens, these being produced principally in the zona fasciculata and zona reticularis in both males and females (Fig. 5-1).

5.2.1 Hydrocortisone

The predominant glucocorticoid varies from species to species and may be cortisol, cortisone or corticosterone. Hydrocortisone (cortisone) is the major glucocorticoid in man and has a plasma half-life of between one and two hours. The glucocorticoids are so-called because they correct defects in carbohydrate metabolism by increasing gluconeogenesis – the sequence of events which leads to the production of glucose or glycogen from amino acids. When excess hydrocortisone is produced (Cushing's syndrome) muscle proteins are broken down and because amino acids are not taken up into muscle as normal there is a net loss of nitrogen from the body. This is seen as muscle wasting. Glucocorticoids also enhanced the mobilization of free fatty acids. Further details of the effects of the glucocorticoids on metabolism are covered in Chapter 10.

Hydrocortisone is necessary for the animal to respond to 'stress'. 'Stress' can be defined as something which threatens the integrity of the animal, for example pain, injury, blood loss, or fear. Hydrocortisone has an additive effect on the actions of aldosterone (a mineralocorticoid) in maintaining plasma fluid volume; it prevents the dilatation of small arterioles and enhances the action of noradrenalin in causing vasoconstriction. Finally there is a direct action to stimulate the force of contraction of the heart. Overall these actions will help prevent blood loss from an injury, maintain plasma volume at the expense of tissue fluid and maintain the blood pressure. The glucocorticoids therefore enable the animal to resist physiological shock more easily.

For many years it has been known that fluid retention occurs following adrenalectomy. This is because the glucocorticoids normally act on the renal tubules, helping to control the rate of fluid loss. In the absence of the glucocorticoids there will be fluid retention. It is likely that glucocorticoids are necessary for aldosterone's action on sodium retention (see below), and they seem essential for the body to eliminate excess sodium.

Hydrocortisone has numerous other actions, the most important of which is its facilitative action – it enables other hormones to work. The other actions are only seen when the glucocorticoid is given in excess and include effects on T4 secretion, gastric secretion and calcium excretion. Actions on the blood cells and anti-inflammatory actions have also been observed. Whether these actions are significant physiologically is not known. However, some have proved useful therapeutically and hydrocortisone is used in the treatment of inflammation.

Hydrocortisone secretion is regulated by ACTH. This effect is rapid and occurs within seconds to minutes. However in the long term ACTH also stimulates growth of the adrenal cortex making more tissue available for hydrocortisone manufacture.

5.2.2 *Aldosterone*

This steroid is produced by the outer zona reticularis of the cortex and acts principally to regulate electrolyte and water metabolism. It is described as a mineralocorticoid in view of its action on minerals such as sodium. It has a half-life of about thirty minutes in plasma.

Aldosterone is taken up by the renal distal tubules and causes an increase in sodium resorption. In exchange for the retention of sodium, potassium and hydrogen ions are lost into the urine. There is a time lag of up to forty minutes before aldosterone brings about this action on the kidney and it seems to affect the active 'sodium pump' as well as affecting sodium permeability.

In addition to its effect on the kidney aldosterone also prevents sodium loss by sweat glands, the salivary glands and the colon. There is possibly also an action on sodium reabsorption in the small intestine. Aldosterone also acts together with ADH to determine the fate of the sodium in the body, to maintain the optimum balance between the sodium and water content of muscle, liver and brain cells. Aldosterone prevents sodium build up in these cells by activating the 'pump' which eliminates the excess.

Aldosterone secretion is controlled mainly by intravascular fluid volume. When the volume falls aldosterone is secreted and this increases sodium retention. Low plasma volume also stimulates thirst, sodium appetite and ADH secretion, and these actions along with the effect of aldosterone lead to fluid retention, so repairing the volume deficit. When the intravascular volume returns to normal, aldosterone secretion drops. The sympathetic nervous system may also directly stimulate aldosterone secretion.

When the blood flow through the kidney falls renin is released and this by a chain of events causes the liberation of angiotensin II which stimulates aldosterone synthesis and secretion (see Chapter 11). The role of other factors in regulating aldosterone secretion is unknown but ACTH, posture and plasma sodium and potassium concentrations might be expected to play a role.

5.3 The adrenal medulla

The cells of the adrenal medulla are embryologically derived from nervous tissue and they are capable of synthesizing catecholamines such as adrenalin and noradrenalin (often called epinephrine and norepinephrine in American texts). In the adult human approximately ten times as much adrenalin as noradrenalin is produced. There appear to be distinct cell types each producing one of the two hormones. Adrenalin is found mainly in the adrenal gland, whereas noradrenalin is a neurotransmitter and is found wherever there are sympathetic nerve terminals.

5.3.1 Adrenalin and noradrenalin

Adrenalin was the first hormone ever to be isolated, crystallized and synthesized. Cannon suggested that the catecholamines were responsible for emergency reactions and the idea of them being necessary for 'fright, fight and flight' is still generally accepted. In response to 'stress' (see definition above) an animal will be frightened and will either wish to fight or flee. Adrenalin will redirect blood to the brain and muscles by appropriate vasodilatation or constriction and increase heart rate and force of contraction. This will facilitate rapid decisions and co-ordinated muscular activity. Blood flow through the liver is increased to allow the outflow of glucose (mobilized from glycogen) to provide a fuel for muscle and brain cells. The bronchial tree is dilated to ensure efficient ventilation and hence an adequate oxygen supply. Blood flow and motility of the intestine and blood flow through the skin is reduced to ensure that the vital organs can work maximally. Humans go white with anger, while in many animals the fur stands on end or they change colour to frighten the adversary. There is also a general state of arousal. The net effect of adrenalin is therefore to prepare for activity – either to fight or to flee.

Noradrenalin tends to counteract these actions in many tissues. Since it is found principally in the sympathetic nervous system it has been suggested that the nervous system can to some extent over-ride the actions of adrenalin.

Based on experiments when noradrenalin and adrenalin were administered to various *in vitro* pharmacological preparations it seems that the actions of noradrenalin must be explained by several receptors. It is generally accepted that for a hormone to work it must activate a tissue receptor. However, depending on the type of tissue and conditions used noradrenalin can have several actions, e.g. causing vasodilatation or vasoconstriction. It has been proposed that activation of one set of receptors causes vasodilatation whilst activation of the other group causes vasoconstriction. The receptors have been designated α and β receptors. In the example cited here activation of the α receptors usually causes vasoconstriction whilst activation of the β receptors usually leads to vasodilatation.

The picture has become extremely complex in recent years with several types of α and β receptors being proposed. For example α_1, α_2, β_1 and β_2 receptors have been identified and others may also exist. Not much is known about the functional significance of these different receptors but each tissue probably contains different receptor populations. Depending on the relative amounts of each receptor type the overall response is determined. It may be that a small concentration of noradrenalin activates for example α_1 receptors while a larger concentration blocks the α_1 receptors and stimulates the α_2 population. As yet we do not clearly understand receptor interaction. However, it is intriguing to speculate that changes in the receptor population at critical times during development, e.g. during pregnancy may explain how noradrenalin can have different effects during different phases of an animals life. Receptor research is a rapidly-growing subject and doubtless some of the complexities of receptor interaction will be unravelled within the next decade.

5.4 Summary

The adrenal gland is a composite gland consisting of a central medulla surrounded by cortical tissue. The cortex is essential for life and produces steroid hormones. The glucocorticoids regulate glucose metabolism and enable the animal to respond to 'stress' in the medium term with effects on fluid balance, and on protein metabolism. They also seem to have facilitative actions. Aldosterone, a mineralocorticoid is necessary for regulation of sodium balance. The adrenal medulla produces the catecholamines noradrenalin and adrenalin, the latter being considered to be important as a circulating hormone. Adrenalin is necessary for the short term response to 'stress' and the fright, fight and flight response. Noradrenalin is principally a neurotransmitter, and its actions have been explained by postulating a number of different receptors.

6 Reproductive Endocrinology I: The Male

Even primitive organisms such as bacteria and the unicellular protozoans show some degree of specialization into two forms that occasionally come together to exchange genetic material. The differences between the two forms may be slight such as the + and − strains of bacteria that look identical, or the differences may be very obvious. The dimorphism of the male drone bee and the enormous female queen is an extreme example. Among the mammals the differences may be less extreme but in most cases the aims are the same − to ensure that members of the same species identify one another and come together to exchange genetic material and rear offspring successfully.

Reproductive physiology is an enormous subject and in the space available it is only possible to emphasize the salient points which are *directly* relevant to endocrinology. In most animals one can identify several stages which the males and females pass through during development. There is a period up until the attainment of sexual maturity followed by gametogenesis (the formation of the ova and sperm), the liberation of the gametes (mating) and finally fertilization and the development of the offspring. In man at least a dozen hormones have a direct role to play during these stages and of course during development all the hormones of metabolism, immunity and growth also come into play.

6.1 The testes

The primary characteristic of the male mammal is the presence of the testes. The two testes (Fig. 6-1) are suspended in a scrotal sac outside the body to keep them at less than 35°C. This is a couple of degrees lower than the temperature of the rest of the body and is essential for normal spermatozoan development. The descent of the testes into the scrotum occurs during intra-uterine life in most mammals and in humans is under the influence of a hormone called human chorionic gonadotrophin (hCG) produced by the placenta in the mother.

Each testis is made up of numerous coiled seminiferous tubules. At the age of puberty, i.e. 12–14 in the human male, LH (ICSH) stimulates the production of testosterone from the interstitial Leydig cells which surround the seminiferous tubules. The testosterone (an androgen, or male sex steroid) brings about the development of the secondary sexual characteristics such as deepening of the voice, the male pattern of bodily hair and the male physical form with broad shoulders, etc. Testosterone is also necessary for seminal fluid production.

FSH stimulates growth of the seminiferous tubules and initiates spermatogenesis. The germinal epithelium produces spermatogonia, and these develop into primary spermatocytes. At this stage a meiosis occurs under the

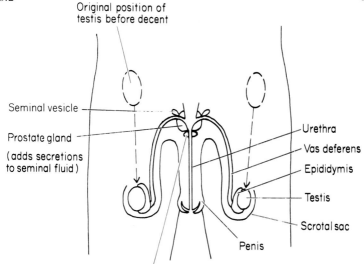

Fig. 6-1   The human male reproductive system.

direct influence of FSH and each primary spermatocyte divides into two secondary spermatocytes, and then four spermatids are formed. A tail develops and four spermatozoa are produced. They obtain nourishment during the later stage of development from the Sertoli cells of the seminiferous tubules (Fig. 6-2).

It has been suggested that under the influence of FSH the Sertoli cells also produce a local hormone and this helps to support spermatogenesis. The evidence for this is sketchy but clearly both FSH and LH (ICSH) are essential for complete spermatogenesis and effective seminal emission. Oestrogens which are produced in small quantities by the testes and the adrenal cortex may also play a supportive role in spermatogenesis.

6.2 Testosterone

In addition to its obvious reproductive functions testosterone is anabolic and so stimulates net protein synthesis. It is because of this action that men are more strongly built than women and have a heavier bone structure. Testosterone may enhance the red blood cell's response to erythropoietin (Chapter 11) and this explains the higher red cell count in males.

The androgenic activity of testosterone leads to stimulation of growth of parts of the genitalia other than the testes. It is therefore responsible for the development and the functioning of the penis, scrotum, prostate gland and seminal vesicles. As described earlier testosterone increases hair growth to give the typical male pattern of beard, chest and abdominal hair, pubic and axillary hair and 'male pattern' baldness. The amount of hair in each individual is

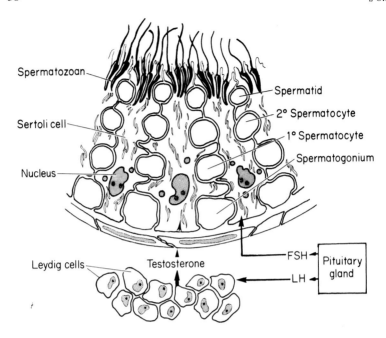

Fig. 6-2 Cross-section of part of one seminiferous tubule showing the sequence of spermatogenesis

determined by the genetic and ethnic pattern of the individual and testosterone acts within these constraints. Testosterone also increases sebum production from the sebaceous glands in the skin, so acne in males is generally worse than that seen in women.

Other 'typical' features of the male, i.e. deep voice, increased muscle mass, aggressive behaviour and high libido (sexual desire) are also caused by testosterone. The aggressive behaviour seems to result from the action of testosterone on the hypothalamus.

Being a steroid testosterone acts on protein synthesis, so its actions are relatively slow but are often of long duration. Testosterone is carried in the plasma bound to a protein called sex hormone binding globulin (SHBG) and so has an effective half-life of several hours.

6.3 Summary

Reproduction in the male is under the influence of three major hormones. FSH and LH (ICSH) promote development of the testes and stimulate and enhance spermatogenesis. Testosterone is produced from the testicular Leydig cells in response to LH (ICSH) and testosterone brings about the secondary sexual characteristics of the male physique, distribution of body hair and deep voice. The male sex drive also seems to be under the influence of testosterone.

7 Reproductive Endocrinology II: The Female

Over the course of evolution the female has become increasingly involved with developing young. In fishes and amphibians fertilization is external and development of the offspring occurs more or less independently of the parents. In reptiles and birds mating occurs and fertilization is internal. The female lays a fertilized egg and development occurs externally. In many reptiles the parents play no further role but in the majority of birds parental behaviour is common. Finally, in the mammals both fertilization and development occur internally and in the placental mammals (i.e. the majority of living mammals) the offspring are born in a reasonably well developed state. In the 'higher' mammals maternal and paternal care extends to the time of sexual maturity of the offspring.

Although this brief account of the evolutionary trend misses out many important exceptions and many exciting individual variations it illustrates how highly developed the mammalian female reproductive system and behaviour have become. Many hormones normally present have a special role to play during the reproductive cycle and at a conservative estimate ten *specific* hormones have evolved each with a role to play in female sexual physiology. The majority of other hormones have their actions modified in some way by the sex hormones.

As in the male we can trace the four distinct stages through which the mammalian female passes during the development to full sexual activity. The attainment of sexual maturity is followed by gametogenesis. The gametes (ova) are then liberated from the ovary and they are fetilized and undergo development within the uterus, a structure developed specifically for this function. The long process towards physical and sexual maturity of the offspring then starts.

7.1 The ovary

The female gonads are the ovaries. The two ovaries (Fig. 7-1) are the primary sexual characteristics of the female. At the time a young mammal is born all the oögonia that will subsequently develop into ova are present in the ovary. In the human these number 200 000 or so. However the oögonia are in an arrested state of development and await the action of FSH from the pubertal pituitary gland. Once initiated oögensis takes several months in the human and a new series of oögonia start developing each month. Many oögonia do not develop successfully; since they have been in arrested development for so many years a large percentage are defective. Only 2–400 functional ova will be produced by the average human in her reproductive life, one usually being produced each month from alternate ovaries. In the polytocous species, i.e.

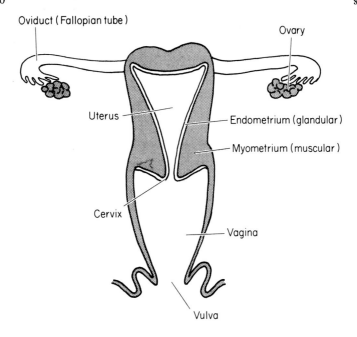

Fig. 7-1   The human ovaries and uterus.

those animals which have many offspring, each ovary produces approximately equal numbers of ova during each sexual cycle.

The process of oögenesis, from oögonium to primary oöcyte, primary follicle and finally the Graafian follicle (Fig. 7-2) requires FSH. When the theca interna of the Graafian follicle has developed it produces an oestrogen. This oestrogen in turn feeds back to the pituitary gland suppressing FSH secretion so reducing further oestrogen secretion. Ovulation is triggered by many factors. These include the transient rise followed by the fall in oestrogen which causes FSH release. The sudden release of LH, possibly in a pulsatile manner, also plays a role and the prostaglandins have been implicated.

Just before ovulation the first meiotic division of the oöcyte occurs and the secondary oöcyte is liberated. The second meiotic division occurs soon after and the ovum passes into the fallopian tube (oviduct) where ciliary movements carry it to the uterus.

The remains of the follicle grow inwards and form a corpus luteum, a dense mass of cells which produce progesterone and oestrogen to maintain the uterine endometrium and so enable pregnancy to occur. The ovary is essential during early pregnancy in the human.

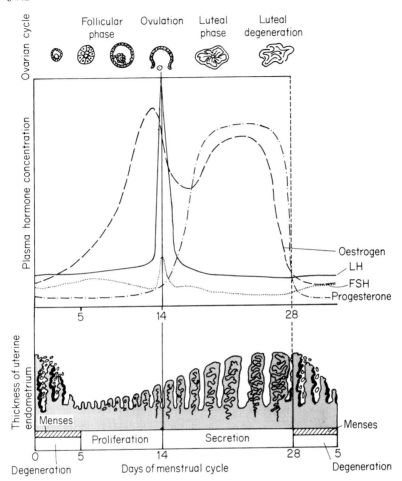

Fig. 7-2   Hormonal changes in the human menstrual cycle and parallel changes in the ovary and uterine endometrium.

7.2 The uterus

The uterus in the human is only about 7.5 cm long and it consists of an outer layer of smooth muscle called the myometrium which encloses the glandular endometrium (Fig. 7-1). The function of the uterus is to accept the fertilized ovum and promote and maintain its development.

The endometrium of the human uterus undergoes cyclical changes under the influence of oestrogens and progesterone (Fig. 7-2). The menstrual cycle starts at menses which is the shedding and re-absorption of much of the endometrial lining. At day 5 with rising levels of oestrogen produced by the theca interna cells of the developing follicle the uterine endometrium is undergoing regeneration and repair. When ovulation has occurred both oestrogen and progesterone are produced by the corpus luteum and under the combined influence of both hormones the endometrium undergoes proliferation. It becomes well vascularized and ready to accept the fertilized ovum. There is some evidence that prolactin also plays a role in the luteal phase of the menstrual cycle.

Fertilization occurs in the fallopian tube and 4–5 days later the ovum enters the uterus. At this stage the uterus is ready to receive the developing ball of cells called a blastocyst. If fertilization has not been successful the corpus luteum regresses and so the uterine endometrium degenerates due to the lack of oestrogenic and progestational support. This regression is brought about by spasm of the spiral arteries in the endometrium. Not all of the endometrium is lost, much is reabsorbed since few animals could afford to waste valuable nutrients. The changes in the uterus together with those occurring simultaneously in the ovary are illustrated in Fig. 7-2.

7.3 Pregnancy

Numerous endocrine changes serve to promote the chance of pregnancy, from the effect of oestrogen and progesterone on the cervical mucosa to ensure only the fittest sperm can pass through, to the cyclical changes responsible for development of an ideal endometrial lining to the uterus. Progesterone and oestrogens control the contractions of the fallopian tube that help to propel the fertilized ovum into the uterus. The developing blastocyst embeds in the endometrium (a process called nidation or implantation) and part of the blastocyst called the trophoblast together with part of the endometrium develop into the placenta. There is evidence that progesterone and oestrogens are essential for implantation and T4 and relaxin (see below) may also play a role.

The chorion, one of the membranes of the placenta, produces at least two polypeptide hormones. The human chorionic gonadotrophin (hCG) maintains the corpus luteum. The human placental lactogen (hPL) which is also luteotrophic together with hCG, takes over the role of LH/FSH in maintaining early pregnancy. In some species a uterine luteolysin (probably prostaglandin $F_{2\alpha}$, $PGF_{2\alpha}$) controls the life span of the corpus luteum. However this has not been unequivocally demonstrated in man. Immunologically pregnancy is a very difficult time, since a 'foreign body' with some of the genetic components of the father is embedded in the uterus. hPL may play a role in suppressing the defence reactions so helping to maintain the pregnancy.

The relative role of the placenta and ovary in maintaining pregnancy and in hormone secretion varies from species to species. However, in man the placenta takes over completely after the first third of pregnancy and is competent in producing sufficient gonadotrophin, lactogen, progesterone and oestrogen. Progesterone maintains the uterine myometrium in a quiescent state while oestrogens counteract this effect. By end of pregnancy the progestogenic component diminishes and regular uterine contractions start. The myometrium is greatly enlarged by the action of these hormones and by the physical stretch caused by the developing foetus. It is now capable of expelling the young child.

7.4 Parturition

The last ten to fifteen years has seen a wealth of research into the factors responsible for parturition. It appears to be a multifactorial process. If one or several of the components described below is absent the others compensate and allow a relatively normal birth to occur. The prime factor initiating parturition appears to be the development of the foetal nervous system and hence the pituitary gland. The adenohypophysis, under hypothalamic control, begins to produce ACTH which acts on the foetal adrenal gland causing it to secrete hydrocortisone. The hydrocortisone is necessary for foetal lung development and explains why premature babies often have breathing difficulties. Hydrocortisone circulates to the placenta where it decreases progesterone secretion and enhances oestrogen production. $PGF_{2\alpha}$ is produced by the uterus and this has a luteolytic action on the ovary in those species where there is an ovarian component in steroid secretion.

Under the influence of high oestrogen and low progesterone, $PGF_{2\alpha}$ can promote uterine activity. $PGF_{2\alpha}$ is probably released in a pulsatile manner and this may add to the regularity of the uterine contractions. The contractions of the uterus push the foetus towards the cervix where pressure initiates Fergussen's reflex (Chapter 2) and so stimulates oxytocin release. A positive feedback loop is therefore initiated.

Pressure on the cervix and the changing ratio of oestrogen to progesterone also seem to initiate the release of a further hormone relaxin. This is a peptide hormone produced in the ovary. Relaxin may play a role in regulating the uterine contractions but in some species it allows the birth canal to relax more readily, hence its name.

Finally with all these positive feedbacks initiated they are self-perpetuating until the child is born. The uterus slowly returns to a relatively quiescent state and the placenta (after-birth) is detached and delivered. Oestrogens promote blood clotting and this helps prevent excessive blood loss at this vulnerable time.

7.5 Lactation

The principal hormones present during pregnancy, i.e. progesterone and oestrogen, together with prolactin, the glucocorticoids, hPL, T4 and insulin, enable the mammary glands to develop full milk yeild soon after birth and oxytocin aids efficient milk release or 'let down' (Chapter 2). Prolactin may also help prevent further ovulation until lactation is complete since the mother's energy is best used to suckle the young which have successfully negotiated the problems of pregnancy rather than to initiate another pregnancy.

7.6 Summary

The secretion and/or the actions of the majority of the hormones in the body undergo some change as a result of reproductive changes, especially during pregnancy. The gonadotrophins prepare the body for sexual life and initiate the secretion of oestrogens and progesterone. These steroids are the principal hormones responsible for preparing for and maintaining pregnancy. The placenta also contributes to a greater or lesser degree in different species, producing gonadotrophins, lactogens and steroid hormones. During pregnancy the various hormones maintain the foetus in an optimal environment and then prepare for the very hazardous event of birth and subsequent lactation. The foetus is the major factor triggering birth but neither it, or any other factor seems to be absolutely essential for a 'normal' birth. Parturition is multifactorial and with numerous standby and back-up mechanisms the chances of success are optimized. After all, this determines the future of the species.

8 Hormones of the Alimentary Canal

The first substances to be called hormones were the two intestinal polypeptides secretin and gastrin. They were discovered in 1902 and 1905 respectively. However, there is still some debate over whether they should be called hormones. For example we do not know whether secretin is produced by all cells of the duodenal mucosa or whether its production is restricted to unicellular glands in this portion of the intestine. There is also some overlap in the actions of these hormones that has made elucidation of their functions difficult.

8.1 Gastrin

Gastrin was discovered in 1905 by Edkins but its presence was disbelieved by many until 1938 when its existence was finally confirmed. Gastrin is a polypeptide consisting of 17 amino acids. It is produced by the mucosa of the pyloric region of the stomach in response to mechanical distention and the local action of various components of food. It is carried the short distance to the fundic region of the stomach in the blood stream where it stimulates the production of hydrochloric acid. Gastrin can also stimulate pancreatic secretion, and this may be explained by the structural similarity to cholecystokinin-pancreozymin.

8.2 Secretin

Secretin was discovered in 1902 by Bayliss and Starling and is now known to be a single chain polypeptide of 27 amino acids, which is chemically similar to glucagon. The exact cellular site of its secretion is not known, though some if not all of the cells of the duodenal mucosa are capable of producing secretin. The stimulus for secretin release is the presence of chyme in the duodenum. It passes in the blood stream to the pancreas where it directly stimulates the acinar cells and initiates the flow of pancreatic juice, but not the release of enzymes. It also stimulates the flow of bile and intestinal juices to some extent. Secretin release is stimulated by the intermediates formed from the breakdown of foods, by hydrochloric acid from the stomach and by alcohol. GH and ACTH play a role in maintaining secretin production, though details of these actions are incomplete.

8.3 Cholecystokinin-pancreozymin

The presence of fat, fatty acids, hydrochloric acid and peptones in the duodenum causes the gall bladder to contract and release its contents. This action is not totally elicited by the nervous system. A hormone called cholecystokinin is released from the intestinal mucosa, though like secretin its exact cellular origin is unclear. A second hormone pancreozymin appears to be released by the mucosa of the upper intestine, its action is complementary to that of secretin in that it stimulates the pancreatic acinar cells to secrete enzymes but does not influence the volume of pancreatic juice. Attempts to separate the activities of pancreozymin and cholecystokinin have proved impossible and it now seems that these are two actions of one hormone now called cholecystokinin-pancreozymin. Chemically this hormone has a number of features in common with gastrin.

8.4 Gastrointestinal glucagon (GI glucagon)

As with secretin the cellular origin of this hormone is not clear, though the duodenum and jejunum are possibly the sites of production, Fig. 8-1. GI glucagon is approximately twice the molecular weight of pancreatic glucagon. It has been suggested that the presence of glucose in the alimentary canal may stimulate GI glucagon release and the GI glucagon then inhibits pancreatic glucagon secretion and stimulates insulin release. Very little is known about this hormone and its significance awaits clarification.

8.5 Summary

Several hormones have been extracted from the alimentary canal and several others have been postulated. Gastrin is produced by the pylorus of the stomach

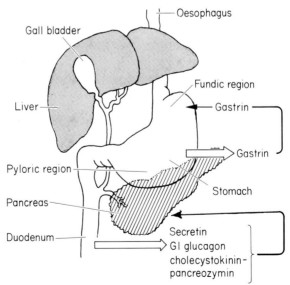

Fig. 8-1 The sites of production of the hormones from the alimentary canal.

and stimulates hydrochloric acid secretion by the fundic region of the gland in response to food and mechanical stimulation. When food is liberated into the duodenum secretin and cholecystokinin-pancreozymin are liberated from the mucosa and stimulate the exocrine pancreas. Secretin stimulates the flow of pancreatic juice while cholecystokinin-pancreozymin initiates enzyme release. GI glucagon may also be liberated by the presence of sugar in the duodenum and appears to suppress pancreatic glucagon release and stimulate insulin production. These actions of the hormones of the alimentary canal are summarized in Fig. 8-1.

9 The Endocrine Pancreas and Diabetes Mellitus

The disease diabetes mellitus, which is characterized by an excessive flow of sugary urine, was first documented over 3500 years ago. In 1562 the term diabetes was used to decribe the disease but over one hundred years elapsed before the sugary nature of the urine was recorded. This was the first documented distinction between diabetes mellitus and diabetes insipidus, where the urine is tasteless (see Chapter 2). Over the following two hundred years the sugar was found to be glucose and Claude Bernard demonstrated the presence of abnormally high concentrations of blood glucose in diabetic patients.

In the late nineteenth century Langerhans described small clusters of cells (the islets of Langerhans) in the pancreas. He noticed that these were well vascularized but unlike the digestive acini did not connect with the duct system of the pancreas. Von Mering and Minkowski later demonstrated that total pancreatectomy led to the symptoms of diabetes mellitus. Subsequently in the 1920s Banting and Best received a Nobel prize for preparing pancreatic islet extracts which could reverse some of the effects of the disease. Insulin has since been crystallized and was the first naturally-occurring protein to be synthesized. Insulin is available for the routine treatment of diabetes mellitus.

9.1 The endocrine pancreas – anatomy and histology

The pancreas is a compound gland located between the duodenum and the liver. It consists of exocrine and endocrine tissues. The exocrine component makes up 98% of the mass of the pancreas and it secretes pancreatic juice which is poured into the duodenum via the pancreatic ducts. There are discrete islets of cells, the pancreatic islets of Langerhans, scattered throughout the exocrine acinar tissue (Fig. 9-1). In the human there may be up to 2 million islets each measuring between 20 and 300 μm in diameter. Within each islet the cells are arranged in irregular chains or cords which are separated by a very rich blood supply – partly blood vessels and partly sinuses. Both exocrine and endocrine pancreatic components are well supplied with nervous tissue.

The islets consist of three types of cells, the α-, β- and δ-cells (D-cells). The α-cells secrete glucagon, and tend to be arranged around the periphery of the islets. The more numerous β-cells produce insulin while the δ-cells probably produce somatostatin which appears to be indentical to GHRIH (Fig. 9-1 and p. 00). Since all three hormones are polypeptides it has been difficult to extract them from the pancreas due to contamination by the proteolytic enzymes in pancreatic juice. For the same reason it has proved difficult to isolate pancreatic islets for *in vitro* work.

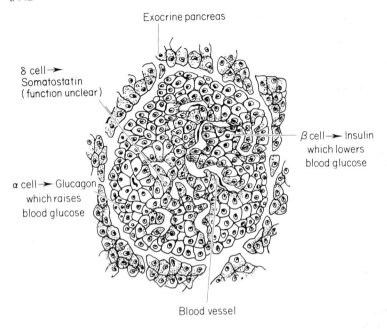

Fig. 9-1 The pancreatic islets of Langerhans and their hormones.

9.2 Insulin

The chemical nature of insulin was determined by Sanger's team between 1945 and 1955 and it was synthesized in 1963. The insulins of different species are similar but not identical. Langerhans discovered follicles of cells in the lowest vertebrates which have since been shown to synthesize insulin and some starfish also produce insulin. Its widespread nature is therefore evident.

Insulin is manufactured as a single chain pro-insulin of about 84 amino acids. The chain is cleaved enzymatically to form an A chain of about 21 amino acids and a B chain of about 30 amino acids – there are species differences in the exact numbers in each chain. Disulphide bridges link the two chains (Fig. 9-2). Identification of which amino acids vary from species to species gives some indication of which parts of the molecule are necessary for biological activity.

Insulin is largely bound to protein carriers in the plasma and it has an effective half-life of between 10 and 15 minutes. The hepatic portal vein carries insulin to the liver where 50% is utilized. Insulin becomes firmly bound to target tissues, being chemically bound to the cells prior to its action.

The action of insulin is to directly stimulate a carrier mediated membrane transport system facilitating glucose uptake into cells, principally muscle cells. It also prevents excessive breakdown of liver and muscle glycogen (glycogenolysis). The action of insulin is therefore hypoglycaemic – it reduces

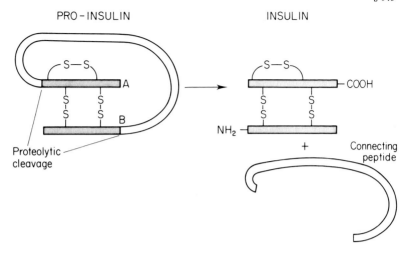

PRO - INSULIN INSULIN

Proteolytic cleavage

Fig. 9-2 Diagrammatic representation of the structure of insulin.

blood glucose. However, it must not be thought that insulin only affects carbohydrate metabolism. Insulin stimulates lipogenesis by promoting the uptake and utilization of glucose by adipose tissue and by preventing lipolysis. It does not stimulate fatty acid uptake since these molecules freely pass across cell membranes. Insulin promotes the entry of amino acids into cells and favours protein synthesis. The net effect of insulin therefore is to store away the food reserves. The major stimulus to the release of insulin is plasma glucose concentrations, though amino acids also stimulate insulin secretion.

9.3 Glucagon

Glucagon is a single chain polypeptide of 29 amino acids. It is chemically unlike insulin. Glucagon is produced from the α-cells of the pancreatic islets and has a plasma half-life of less than 10 minutes.

The principal action of glucagon is to raise blood glucose concentrations. This is brought about by stimulating glycogen breakdown in the liver and within 1–2 minutes this increases blood glucose. Glucagon also stimulates gluconeogenesis. As the name implies this is the process which produces new glucose, from liver protein, amino acids and pyruvic acid. This is a more lengthy process and glucose from this source is not available for 30 minutes after activation by glucagon.

In addition to its effect on carbohydrate metabolism glucagon also stimulates lipolysis in adipose tissue to liberate fatty acids. These are then available to the liver and muscle for catabolism and hence energy production. The effect is to supply glucose where needed, e.g. the brain, but also to make fatty acids available as an alternative energy supply where glucose is not essential. Finally, when present in large quantities glucagon has an overall effect on protein degradation, presumably to liberate the amino acids for gluconeogenesis – but only when absolutely necessary.

The overall effect of glucagon is to counter the effects of insulin on metabolism, though there are some sites where one or other acts alone. For example glucagon has no effect on glucose uptake into cells. A delicate balance between the two hormones is normally present so that there is a fine and rapid control of metabolism. Indeed it seems likely that glucagon acts mildly to stimulate the secretion of insulin to ensure that there is always a basal level of insulin in the blood, so preventing the onset of diabetes mellitus.

The duodenum and jejunum produce GI glucagon, a completely separate hormone from pancreatic glucagon. It has been suggested that the presence of glucose in the alimentary canal stimulates the release of GI glucagon. The GI glucagon then circulates to the pancreatic β-cells to stimulate insulin release. Therefore, insulin is available to store away the glucose as soon as it enters the circulation.

The control of pancreatic glucagon secretion is by plasma glucose and possibly fatty acids. GI glucagon may inhibit pancreatic glucagon secretion. A further gastro-intestinal hormone cholecystokinin-pancreozymin which is stimulated by the presence of amino acids in the alimentary canal, may stimulate pancreatic glucagon secretion.

9.4 Diabetes mellitus

The overall roles of insulin and glucagon are to maintain a balance between the storage of food and its release when and where required. The disease diabetes mellitus is characterized by the presence of glucose in the urine and this is due to a defect in the pancreatic β-cells which produce insulin. This may be a hereditary defect which becomes evident before the age of 30 years or it may occur later in life due to the progressive failure of the β-cells. However, although the primary defect is in the β-cells or in some cases in the ability to respond to insulin, diabetes causes widespread vascular damage and there is no clear evidence that the control of diabetes with insulin can reverse this damage. More people die or are made ill by the secondary effects of the disease than by the direct results of insulin deficiency.

The normal adult blood sugar concentration is kept at a relatively steady 80 mg per 100 ml of blood (4.5 mMol l^{-1}), i.e. we each have approximately 1 teaspoonful of sugar available for immediate use. In diabetes insulin maybe (*i*) absent, (*ii*) present in only small quantities or (*iii*) the β-cells respond only slowly to stimulation by glucose. Therefore when we ingest glucose in our diet the blood glucose concentration rises since insufficient insulin is present to supervise its storage. When the glucose rises above 180 mg per 100 ml of blood (10 mMol l^{-1}) it exceeds the renal threshold and glucose 'spills' out into the urine – hence the well-known defect, sugar in the urine. Therefore the disease has been described as 'starvation amidst plenty' since the valuable glucose is wasted. In order to remove the excess sugar in solution the urine volume increases and hence the patient becomes thirsty. In the absence of available food he may also be hungry. These symptoms will be present in the severe cases of the disease. All or few of the symptons are present in each individual since diabetes mellitus covers a range of conditions varying from mild to very severe. The following discussion describes the changes occurring in the total absence of insulin – when some insulin is present these changes will occur, but to a milder degree.

In the absence of insulin glucose enters muscle and liver cells very slowly. However, since there is no insulin to stimulate the synthesis of glycogen in the liver to store the sugar, the glycogen is quickly metabolized. This might not seem too disastrous since there is plenty of fat in the diet which is rich in energy. However, the brain has an absolute requirement for glucose as its energy supply if it is to function normally. It requires over 400 kcal day^{-1} (1680 kJ day^{-1}, i.e. 20% of our daily energy intake, all in the form of glucose. Fortunately insulin is not necessary for the cells of the nervous system to take up glucose.

Since the glucose is being lost in the urine because of the lack of insulin, adipose tissue is used as a source of energy. Therefore fatty acids are released into the blood. It is the metabolism of the fatty acids that ultimately causes the diabetic coma. The fatty acids are inadequately metabolized and produce ketone bodies. This gives the characteristic 'pear drops' smell to the breath of patients suffering from ketosis. The brain can be damaged by using this improper energy source. The ketones are acidic and they lower the blood pH – this depresses respiration and damages nervous tissue. An equally damaging effect of acidity in the diabetic is its partial inhibition of glucose utilization by muscle. Finally an acidotic coma ensues which if untreated leads to death. In the early stages glucose can reverse the symptoms before too much brain damage is caused.

Fortunately purified insulin is now available. Being a protein it has to be administered by injection and cannot be taken by mouth because of the proteolytic enzymes in the alimentary canal. A mixture of rapid and long-acting preparations is often used to control glucose metabolism for about 8–12 hours. This means that insulin must be administered twice daily. However, not all diabetics require insulin. A careful diet or the use of drugs to stimulate the β-cells is often adequate if some insulin is still present.

This description of diabetes mellitus is by necessity very brief and many important points have been skimmed over. Many thick volumes have been written on just the metabolic effects of the disease. However, it does serve to show how a defect in one cell type, the pancreatic β-cell, can have devastating effects on life. An understanding of endocrinology and metabolism has enabled doctors to treat the disease in the many millions of patients (up to 2% of the population) who suffer from just one of the forms of diabetes mellitus.

9.5 Summary

The pancreas consists of endocrine and exocrine components. The endocrine pancreas is made up of 1–2 million islets of Langerhans which produce glucagon (α-cells), insulin (β-cells), and somatostatin (D- or δ-cells). Insulin helps to store glucose, amino acids and fatty acids away whilst glucagon is antagonistic to these actions. The fine balance between the two hormones maintains a fairly stable blood glucose concentration. When the pancreatic β-cells are defective diabetes mellitus (sugar diabetes) is caused to a greater or lesser extent.

In diabetes mellitus glucose cannot be adequately stored and it is lost in the urine. The brain is forced to use fatty acid breakdown products called ketones as a source of energy and this causes metabolic acidosis and ultimately death following a coma. The symptoms of diabetes can be controlled in many patients by appropriate diet, drugs to stimulate the β-cells or with injections of insulin.

10 The Hormonal Control of Metabolism

Some animals, particularly the herbivores, spend a great deal of their life eating. However other animals eat only very irregularly and must take the opportunity to feed when it arises. The carnivores are examples of the latter group and many go for days or even weeks without feeding. Obviously these animals must be able to store away the energy and nutrients from their irregular meals and be able to gradually liberate the energy whilst they await their next opportunity to eat. Hibernating animals to a certain extent have a similar problem.

Man, being an omnivore, falls some way between the typical herbivore and typical carnivore – eating several times a day. Nevertheless it is essential to be able to store away food when it arrives, ensuring enough is available for immediate needs and then to slowly release the food at the correct site in the body when required. It is therefore essential to be able to control metabolism. At least six different hormones play a role in regulating metabolism.

10.1 Sites of action of hormones affecting metabolism

The metabolism of the three major groups of food, i.e. carbohydrates, fats and proteins, is regulated by hormones. However, each is affected mainly at only one or two key sites.

The uptake of carbohydrates into cells and the enzymes affecting carbohydrate storage are regulated by hormones (Fig. 10-1). Insulin stimulates glucose entry into cells and stimulates the glycogen synthetase enzyme responsible for the conversion of glucose-6-phosphate to glycogen, the storage product. Glucagon and adrenalin counteract the latter action by affecting the glycogen phosphatase enzyme. These effects on the glycogen phosphatase and synthetase enzymes are brought about by a complex series of reactions.

Amino acid uptake into cells is stimulated by growth hormone (GH) and insulin, and it is retarded by the glucocorticoids (GC) such as hydrocortisone (Fig. 10-1). GH acts with insulin to stimulate some of the enzymes responsible for protein synthesis while the GCs have the converse action.

Fatty acids are freely permeable across cell membranes and hormones do not seem to affect this process. However, insulin stimulates the triglyceride synthetase enzyme which catalyses the conversion of glycerol and free fatty acids into fat in adipose tissue (Fig. 10-1). Glucagon, adrenalin and GCs activate the triglyceride lipase enzyme that liberates the free fatty acids and glycerol from fat. T4 seems to aid the catabolic (breaking down) actions of many of the hormones.

The hormones regulating metabolism act at membrane sites by activating

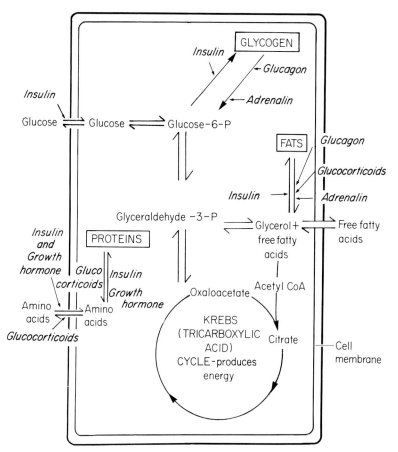

Fig. 10-1 Diagrammatic representation of a 'generalized' cell to show where the major hormones act in the control of metabolism. Some reactions predominate in one cell type whereas others occur principally in other types of cells.

transport mechanisms or at key enzyme sites by activating the enzymes. In the long term, however, the GCs and GH will cause the manufacture of more enzyme molecules or new enzyme species.

In this chapter some of the major metabolic changes that occur in man are outlined and the effects on metabolism at the above sites will be considered. It should be appreciated that this is a very sketchy outline and many books are available should you wish to pursue this fascinating subject further. Figure 10-1 shows the key sites where metabolism is regulated in a generalized cell – some of these reactions will predominate in one cell type, e.g. glycogen metabolism in the liver, whereas others are present mainly in other tissues, e.g. lipid metabolism in adipose tissue. The illustration is purely to help visualize where the hormones act.

10.2 Eating

In a normal balanced diet we ingest carbohydrates, fats and proteins. These are digested in the alimentary canal and are absorbed as their component parts, i.e. sugars such as glucose, fatty acids and glycerol, and amino acids.

Soon after eating the blood glucose concentration rises and since we usually take in more glucose than is required, it is necessary to store the majority of this. The GI glucagon and raised blood glucose stimulate insulin release and the insulin enhances peripheral glucose uptake and lipolysis – much of the glucose being stored as fat. The high blood glucose suppresses GH release, and seems to decrease the effect of adrenalin on lipolysis. The free fatty acids absorbed in a meal enter cells well and under the action of insulin, as described above, will tend to be stored as fat. The amino acids absorbed must be quickly diverted to use in protein synthesis if they are not to be metabolized. Like glucose they stimulate insulin release and insulin stimulates their uptake into tissues and incorporation into protein. The amino acids also stimulate GH release; the quantity of this hormone in the blood therefore depends on the balance of nutrients in the diet. GH, in combination with insulin, stimulates protein synthesis.

10.3 Postprandial changes

The blood glucose usually returns to normal about two hours after eating, and at this point there is less insulin and more GH present in the blood. During this transition period lipolysis is still inhibited since the triglyceride lipase is very sensitive to low levels of insulin. Protein synthesis continues.

10.4 Mild starvation

Probably up to 75% of our life is spent in starvation since this is the period approximately two hours after eating until our next meal. During mild starvation blood glucose and amino acid levels are falling slowly whilst the free fatty acids are gradually liberated from their store. The fall in blood glucose blocks insulin release and stimulates the release of GH, adrenalin and glucagon. From Fig. 10-1 it can be seen that these changes will cause glycogenolysis in the liver, degrading glycogen to compensate for the fall in blood glucose. Lipolysis will also occur to liberate fatty acids. Meanwhile some protein synthesis will still continue under the influence of GH until amino acid levels become too low.

10.5 Extreme starvation

If the next meal does not occur when expected the mild starvation tends towards extreme starvation and the changes in glycogenolysis and lipolysis outlined above will be exaggerated. We have only a limited supply of glycogen in the liver and this is quickly exhausted. Glycogen synthesized from fatty acids can be mobilized as glucose. However, eventually many of the changes seen in diabetes mellitus will occur and ketone production will start. However, the small amounts of insulin present probably prevent this occurring to any great extent. In long-term starvation (more than six to eight hours) GCs, the hormones of long term stress, are mobilized and it will be evident from Fig. 10-1 that these promote proteolysis and enhance lipolysis. T4 probably plays a role here in aiding lipolysis. In this state of starvation the hormonal changes which support the blood glucose tend to direct the glucose away from the muscle and to the brain. It will be recalled from Chapter 9 that the brain must have glucose to function normally.

One essential effect of starvation is to increase the appetite. What causes this is unknown, though it has been suggested that GH may play a role. Eating has a very potent action in reversing the effects of starvation.

10.6 Exercise and 'stress'

Exercise causes a very rapid fall in blood glucose and free fatty acids because of their rapid utilization. Within ten minutes lipolysis is stimulated so that fatty acids can be used by muscle as a source of energy. It is probable that adrenalin and possibly a fall in plasma insulin levels can account for these changes. T4 increases the sensitivity to adrenalin and may also play a role here.

'Stress' such as cold, fear, injury, etc., stimulates the nervous system and causes adrenalin release in the short term. Subsequently GH and GCs are released so liberating energy in the form of fatty acids to enable the immediate stress to be dealt with. T4 is also elevated and the combination of these hormones will help the body to cope with the potential threat.

In both exercise and stress the catecholamines help to liberate glucose from glycogen to enable the brain to maintain its essential supply of energy to help co-ordinate and cope with the particular demands of the exercise or stress.

10.7 Summary

Insulin plays an essential role in regulating the changes following food intake, and adrenalin probably plays a similar role following exercise or stress. The other hormones that help to mobilize and store food as and where necessary are glucagon, GH, T4, and the GCs. The overall aim is to store most of the food immediately after a meal and to release it gradually as and when necessary. This ensures that the animal can stay alive between meals and have sufficient rapidly available energy to cope with the stress of possible injury or with the exercise entailed when, for example, chasing the prey.

11 Miscellaneous Endocrine Glands and Tissue Hormones

11.1 The thymus gland

The thymus gland is a small ductless gland which varies in size in different animal species. It is found in the neck of juveniles and in many species it disappears relatively soon after birth. In rodents the gland is present into adult life and these animals have provided evidence for the function of the gland. When thymectomy is performed soon after birth the ability to respond to antigens by producing antibodies is greatly reduced. However, the same operation in adult rodents does not impair their immune functions, though there is a fall in the number of lymphocytes. The thymus gland appears to produce lymphocyte stem cells which migrate to the peripheral lymphoid tissues. The thymus also produces thymus hormone which stimulates the lymphocytes and renders them capable of producing antibody-producing cells and so participating in immune reactions. What factors control the thymus and details of the actions of the thymus hormone are not yet clear but this area is a focus of research and will doubtless reveal a considerable amount of fascinating information during the next decade.

11.2 The parathyroid glands and the parafollicular cells

There are usually four small parathyroid glands in the neck of man and they were identified in the middle of the last century. It was shown that removal of the thyroid gland and hence the parathyroid glands which are closely attached often resulted in tetany. This is a condition where the muscles fail to function due to inadequate calcium supplies. Subsequently a parathyroid hormone (parathormone, PTH), a polypeptide of 84 amino acids, has been identified and chemically purified. PTH is synthesized in large quantities for such a small gland and is produced only when required, very little being stored in the gland. It has a half-life of about 20 minutes in the peripheral circulation.

Embedded in the thyroid gland are some lightly staining cells called the parafollicular cells (Fig. 4-1). In the early 1960s it was realized that a calcium lowering agent was produced by these cells. This hormone is called thyrocalcitonin (TCT) or calcitonin. Only eight years after its discovery the hormone was synthesized. It is a polypeptide of 32 amino acids and has a short plasma half-life of between five and fifteen minutes.

It is now known that PTH tends to raise blood calcium and TCT acts to lower it. However, the metabolism of magnesium and phosphate are closely connected with calcium. It seems likely the PTH and TCT are involved with their metabolism also, and that together with vitamin D, which some people would consider to be a hormone, PTH and TCT maintain the fine control of the distribution of these minerals between bone, tissues and body fluids.

11.3 The kidney

Although the major function of the kidney is to regulate the water and ionic balance of the body there is growing evidence that it is also an important endocrine gland. Like many tissues the kidney produces prostaglandins (see section 11.5). Prostaglandin E_2 (PGE_2) has been known for some time and was originally called medullin before its chemical nature was known. It appears to block the action of ADH on water resorption.

The kidney also produces erythropoietin which stimulates red blood cell production by the bone marrow. This is a very productive area of research but details of the actions and control of erythropoietin are still rather sketchy.

The third hormone produced by the kidney is renin. This has been the focus of considerable research in the last decade. Renin is produced by the juxtaglomerular apparatus which consists of specialized cells of the afferent and efferent glomerular arterioles and by the macula densa – cells of the distal tubule located close to the juxtaglomerular apparatus (Fig. 11-1). This complex of cells probably acts together in the autoregulation of renal blood flow. The cells produce renin when the blood pressure falls and renin raises the blood pressure, ensuring that there is adequate perfusion pressure for renal functioning.

Renin acts on a cascade process (Fig. 11-2a) which converts the renin substrate into angiotensin I and this is converted to angiotensin II, a very potent vasoconstricter hormone with a half-life of about two minutes. Renin

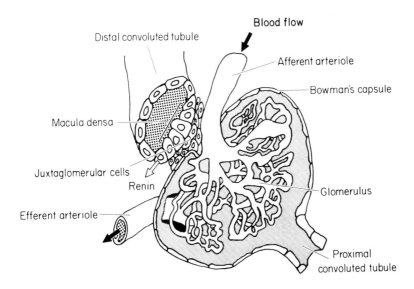

Fig. 11-1   The juxtaglomerular apparatus of the kidney consisting of specialized cells of the afferent and efferent arterioles and the macula densa, specialized cells of the distal tubule.

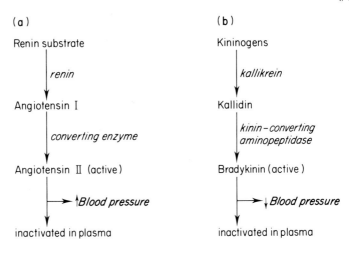

Fig. 11-2 (a) The renin-angiotensin cascade. (b) The kallikrein-kinin cascade.

and angiotensin II directly cause an increase in both sodium and water absorption. Angiotensin II also stimulates aldosterone secretion and so helps to retain sodium via this route.

11.4 The pineal gland

The pineal gland is a small structure which develops from the roof of the 'tween brain. In many species it is orgnized like an eye, with photosensitive cells and a primitive lens-like structure which may be capable of focusing light. Indeed the cranium is very thin over this region of the brain in many species. It is not surprising that this 'third eye' has developed a considerable amount of mythology; during the last century it was considered to be the seat of the rational soul. It is now known that the gland produces serotonin (5–hydroxy tryptamine, 5–HT) which is enzymatically converted to melatonin. There is a diurnal rhythm in the release of melatonin and in some species light affects secretion.

In frogs melatonin causes the skin to lighten and so counteracts the action of MSH. At night when melatonin secretion decreases the skin darkens. Melatonin also serves to control the seasonal colour changes in the weasel.

Numerous regulatory roles of pineal extracts have been ascribed and it is possible that this gland is another structure which helps to co-ordinate nervous and endocrine functions. Its extracts have been shown to regulate thyroid secretion, aldosterone and glucocorticoid secretion and reproductive cycles. Both serotonin and melatonin appear to be biologically active. We must await further experimentation before the role of this gland is clarified.

11.5 'Tissue hormones'

In mammals there are numerous recognized endocrine glands each with their own specific secretions. However, there also seem to be a number of substances that have hormone-like actions but do not appear to emanate from one specific gland or cell type. Many tissue hormones have local actions.

Kinins The kinins (bradykinin, kallidin, and possibly others) are a group of chemically-related peptides of nine to eleven amino acids. They should not be confused with the plant hormones of the same name. All the kinins are formed from common precursors called kininogens which are large molecular weight proteins. A hydrolytic enzyme kallikrein cleaves the kininogen to produce the kinin (Fig. 11-2b). The similarity to the cascade described above for the renin-angiotensin system has not gone unnoticed but awaits explanation. The sites of production of the different components in the cascade are unknown, though the kallikrein is produced by some of the leucocytes in the blood.

The physiological functions of the kinins which circulate in the blood are not yet known. However, they are very potent stimulants of smooth muscle contraction and act equally well on intestinal, venous and bronchial tissues. However they cause dilatation of arteries. The kinins increase the stroke volume of the heart, increase capillary permeability, increase the speed with which leucocytes migrate to the site of injury and cause the sensation of pain in damaged tissues. It has been proposed that the kinins may regulate tissue blood flow and they may play a role in the inflammatory response. There does not yet seem to be a unifying concept to explain the actions of the kinins.

Prostaglandins Although discovered at the beginning of this century the prostaglandins (PGs) have only been intensively researched over the last decade and a half. They are 20-carbon fatty acids and each has the same basic chemical skeleton. Numerous classes of prostaglandins have been identified and the biologically important ones seem to be prostaglandins E, F, A and I. Even these have been subdivided and we have for example $PGF_{2\alpha}$ and PGE_1.

Originally prostaglandins were found in reproductive tissues, they were found in abundance in the prostate gland – hence the name. They are now known to be present in almost all tissues studied. It is clear that they are locally active since they are almost totally inactivated by a single circuit through the lungs. The liver is also very potent as an inactivator in this respect.

The prostaglandins seem to act at two levels. (1) Between glands: for example uterine prostaglandins probably cause regression of the ovarian corpora lutea, and (2) within cells: they may act to regulate cellular chemistry in a manner similar to the way in which cyclic AMP acts as a second messenger in controlling hormone activity. It has been proposed that different prostaglandins may regulate cyclic AMP production and so modulate hormone activity.

11.6 Summary

This chapter has covered many hormones about which little is known and shows some of the areas of endocrinology which are being most intensively researched at the present. It is likely that in the future we will understand better how each of these hormones integrates with the whole mammalian endocrine system.

12 Invertebrate Hormones

The study of invertebrate hormones has lagged some way behind the study of the endocrine system in mammals. However the presence of insect hormones has been known for years; in the 1920s it was shown that insect pupation was under hormonal control. Sir Vincent Wiggleworth was one of the pioneers of the study of insects in the 1940s and 1950s and he undoubtedly stimulated others to work with this prolific and diverse group of animals.

There are obvious problems with the study of invertebrates and these clearly hindered early research. The most obvious limitation is the small size of many invertebrates, making surgery a very demanding task. However, numerous ingenious techniques have been developed over the last forty years, which have demonstrated that many of the processes controlled by hormones in mammals are also subject to endocrine regulation in the invertebrates.

In many invertebrates a large component of the endocrine system is associated with neurosecretion and modified nervous tissue produces circulating hormones (see Chapter 2). Metabolism, reproduction, digestive and excretory processes have all been shown to have an endocrine component. However, many invertebrates have problems not evident in mammals, for example the need for metamorphosis. This was one of the first processes to be shown to be under hormonal control.

12.1 Insect hormones

The endocrine system of insects has been studied extensively. The system consists of neurosecretory cells at the anterior of the brain which connect via nerve axons to the corpora cardiaca (singular corpus cardiacum, literally the 'heart bodies') in the thorax (Fig. 12-1). The corpora cardiaca act as reservoirs for the neurosecretory peptide hormone, and it is released when required.

This peptide acts on the corpora allata, which lie on each side of the gut, causing the release of juvenile hormone (JH). JH normally maintains the juvenile form of the body at the moult, so the insect moults for example from larval stage 2 to larval stage 3. However, the neurosecretory hormone from the corpora cardiaca also acts on the thoracic glands stimulating the release of the steroid moulting hormone, ecdysone, which acts on the epidermis. At moulting ecdysome causes the epidermis to produce the adult cuticle. The balance between JH and ecdysone determines the time of onset of the adult form, and the amount of JH produced probably decreases with successive moults (Fig. 12-1).

Ecdysone is a steroid and has been shown to act by promoting protein synthesis. It acts directly on the chromosomes and like all steroids takes some

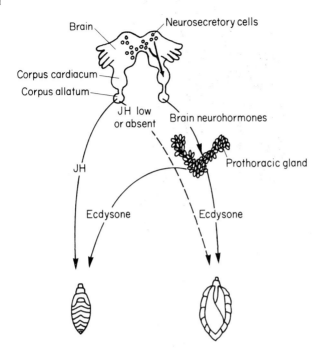

Fig. 12-1 The insect endocrine system and the hormones responsible for moulting.

hours to act. JH is a polypeptide and so acts rapidly through the cyclic AMP mechanism.

The experimental evidence for the endocrine control of moulting and the development of the adult form comes from many experiments. Ligation between the larval brain and thorax was shown to block metamorphosis, suggesting that a blood-borne component was involved with metamorphosis. Numerous experiments were performed by Wigglesworth with the blood-sucking bug *Rhodnius*. *Rhodnius* has been a valuable experimental tool since it moults a fixed time after a blood meal. It is likely that distention of the gut with blood stimulates the moult. Wigglesworth joined two *Rhodnius* larva in 'parabiosis' by connecting their blood supplies together with a fine glass capillary (Fig. 12-2). Feeding one insect before the parabiotic union caused both to moult at the appropriate time. If a final stage larva was connected to a younger larva and the older larva was fed, both assumed the adult form at moulting, one being precocious. Precocious adults could also be produced by allectomy, and the development of the adult form could be delayed by extirpation of the thoracic glands. These elegant experiments and many others demonstrated that there are blood-borne components which stimulate moulting and that can control the type of cuticle which developes. JH and

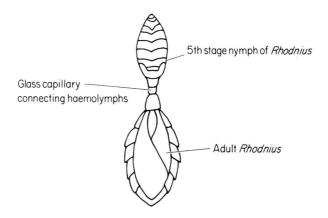

5th stage nymph of *Rhodnius*

Glass capillary
connecting haemolymphs

Adult *Rhodnius*

Fig. 12-2 Insect parabiotic union. The haemocoels of the two insects are joined to demonstrate that a process is controlled by a blood-borne factor.

ecdysone have since been characterized. It has been proposed that JH could be used as a pesticide, to promote the development of adults who are sexually immature and so incapable of reproduction.

Research in the last decade has demonstrated an insect diuretic hormone. This hormone seems to be produced by the neurosecretory cells of some insects and by cells of the ventral nerve cord of others. The hormone acts directly on the Malpighian tubules (the insect organs of excretion) and its action may be balanced by an antidiuretic hormone from the corpora cardiaca in some species.

The attainment of sexual maturity and the development of sexual behaviour in male and female insects appears to be partly hormonally controlled. JH appears to be responsible and it also has effects on fat metabolism. Glucose and protein synthesis also appear to be under hormonal control. Some insects are capable of morphological colour changes and a hormone from the corpora allata appears to be responsible. It is not clear whether this is JH.

12.2 Crustacean hormones

The regulatory mechanisms of crustaceans are very complex and have been extensively studied. The principal endocrine structures are shown in Fig. 12-3. As with insects there are (1) neurosecretory structures, (2) sites of storage of the neurosecretions which possibly modify the secretion and (3) true endocrine glands that release their hormones into the blood. The neurosecretory organs are the X organs. These are located in the eyestalks in species with stalked eyes or in the head in other species. There are also clusters of neurosecretory cells in the brain, the thoracic ganglia and in other sites in the nervous system. Ablation of the eyestalks has demonstrated the neurosecretory role in these structures and more recently very delicate surgical procedures have confirmed the other sites of neurosecretion. The sinus glands are the storage sites for the neurosecretions from the X organs but they may possibly have a secretory role also. They are therefore analogous to the corpora cardiaca of the insects. The Y glands, the androgenic glands (found in males and females), and the ovaries are true endocrine glands under the control of the neurosecretory hormone from the X organs.

Moulting is used as a method of growth in crustaceans in much the same way as in insects. The protective exoskeleton must be moulted to allow an increase in size. As in the insects this is an outward expression of a whole complex of major metabolic adjustments involving the co-ordination of many bodily functions. Experimentally by ablation of the eyestalks, re-implantation, preparation of extracts, etc., it has been shown that the X glands produce a hormone that inhibits moulting. It is stored in the sinus gland. A second antagonistic factor may also be produced in the eyestalk but this remains uncharacterized. However it seems unnecessary to postulate the presence of a moulting hormone from the eyestalk since the Y glands stimulate moulting. It is probable that the neurosecretion is stored in the X glands and is released into the blood where it modulates the release of the moulting hormone from the Y gland (Fig. 12-3). As in the insects a balance between the two hormones controls moulting.

The hormonal control of reproduction appears to be controlled by the ovaries and androgenic glands (not the testes). Neurosecretions from the X gland inhibit ovarian maturation and the secretory activity of the androgenic glands. The Y organ moulting hormone may also be essential for normal ovarian and testicular differentiation. The ovaries and androgenic glands control the sexual characteristics but details of their hormonal secretions are still rather sketchy.

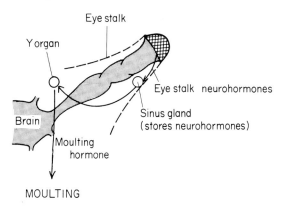

Fig. 12-3 The crustacean endocrine system and the hormones responsible for moulting.

The endocrine control of metabolism in crustaceans seems to be under the influence of the eyestalk neurohormones. Blood sugars, fatty acids and amino acids are well regulated. Other factors under hormonal control appear to be the regulation of heart rate by a substance from the pericardial organs and the regulation of colour changes under the control of the eyestalk neurohormones.

12.3 Other invertebrates

Although a considerable amount of research effort has focused on the insect and crustacean hormones there is growing evidence that hormones are present in all but the most simple invertebrates. Neurosecretory cells are present in the flatworms, annelids and molluscs. Each group seems to have hormonal control over growth and/or regeneration, reproduction and possibly metabolism. The cells responsible are not always located in the head but in some cases they are situated in the nerve cord. It is now possible to explain, for example, the regeneration of damaged earth worms from a small part of their body.

12.4 Pheromones

Not all chemicals produced by invertebrates and vertebrates act in the same organism. Although strictly speaking these are not hormones they are very interesting and worthy of a mention. The general term pheromone has been adopted to describe these chemicals. They affect members of the same species only.

Pheromones are usually very potent. For example a pheromone produced by the female silk moth *Bombyx mori* can be detected by males up to a mile away. This ensures that the moths can locate one another prior to mating. Another pheromone 'queen factor' is produced by the queen bee and this inhibits sexual development of the other females in the colony. However, when the colony becomes too large the queen factor will be diluted and a secondary queen may develop elsewhere in the colony. Death of the queen will have a similar effect. It seems that most pheromones are concerned with sexual activity and some research points to the presence of vertebrate and even mammalian pheromones. The menstrual acitivity of young women in a closed community such as a college hostel has been shown to become co-ordinated to a remarkable degree. Pheromones have tentatively been implicated.

12.5 Summary

Hormones have been found in many very primitive animals. Most animals seem to have neurosecretory mechanisms controlling true endocrine structures. The endocrine control of growth and development, sexual reproduction and metabolism is almost universal and it is likely that the regulation of water balance will also be found to be widespread. Experimental techniques used with vertebrates need adaptation and often rather more refined technical skills are necessary to study invertebrates, but this field presents a fascinating and challenging area of research.

Further Reading

AUSTIN, C.R. and SHORT R.V. (1972). *Reproduction in Mammals Series*, Book 3. Cambridge University Press, Cambridge.

AUSTIN, C.R. and SHORT, R.V. (1980). *Reproduction in Mammals Series*, Book 4. Mechanisms of Hormone Action. Cambridge University Press, Cambridge.

DENTON, R.M. and POGSON, C.I. (1976). *Metabolic Regulation*. Chapman and Hall, London.

DONOVAN, B.T. (1970). *Mammalian Endocrinology*. McGraw-Hill, London.

HARDY, R.N. (1981). *Endocrine Physiology*. Edward Arnold, London.

HARDY, R.N. (1983). *Homeostasis*. Second Edition. Studies in Biology Series, no. 63. Edward Arnold, London.

HIGHNAM, K.C. and HILL, L. (1977). *The Comparative Endocrinology of the Invertebrates*, Second Edition. Edward Arnold, London.

SAWIN, C.T. (1969). *The Hormones*. Endocrine Physiology. Little, Brown & Co. Boston.

TURNER, C.D. and BAGNARA, J.T. (1971). *General Endocrinology*. W.B. Saunders & Co. Philadelphia.

Index